/ U. S. Laws, statutes, etc.

THE
NEW FEDERAL RULES
OF EVIDENCE,
Annotated

With an Analysis by
Paul F. Rothstein
Professor of Law
Georgetown University Law Center

The Bureau of National Affairs, Inc. ● Washington, D.C. 20037

Copyright © 1975
The Bureau of National Affairs, Inc.
Washington, D.C. 20037

KF
8931.5
1975b

Printed in the United States of America
Library of Congress Catalog Card Number: 75-10794
International Standard Book Number: 0-87179-218-4

CANISIUS COLLEGE LIBRARY
BUFFALO, N. Y.

Table of Contents

Analysis

by Paul F. Rothstein

The Federal Rules of Evidence, effective July 1, 1975, represent more than a decade of effort to produce a uniform code of evidence for federal courts. The code was to replace the welter of complexity, diversity, and confusion spawned by Federal Rule of Civil Procedure 43 (a) (which sent the federal courts to state evidence law when no federal evidence statute or equity practice supplied a more liberal rule) and Federal Rule of Criminal Procedure 26 (which mandated federal courts to develop their own criminal evidence rules as federal common law).

"Official" recognition of the need for a new evidence code came in 1961, when the Judicial Conference of the United States reported that a uniform code of evidence for the federal courts was desirable.[1] In 1965, under the auspices of the Conference and the Chief Justice of the United States, an Advisory Committee was appointed to begin drafting rules.[2] The Committee was comprised of a wide cross-section of lawyers, judges, and scholars. In November 1972, after circulation of preliminary drafts, the final Advisory Committee draft was promulgated by the Supreme Court, to become effective July 1, 1973, unless Congress exercised a veto.[3] In March 1973, Congress suspended the effective date of the Rules in order to evaluate them thoroughly.[4] This call for evaluation was largely the result of dissatisfaction with the privilege rules—particularly with their emasculation of state privilege law, restriction of personal privileges, and expansion of governmental privilege.

The Federal Rules of Evidence thereafter went through several congressional drafts and were finally signed into law on February 2, 1975. Cases begun on or after July 1, 1975, will be governed by the Rules. The Court will have power to exempt pending cases where serious inequity would result.

---

[1] Report, 30 F.R.D. 73 (1962).

[2] See transmittal letter, Preliminary Draft of Federal Rules of Evidence, 46 F.R.D. 161 (1969).

[3] The preliminary drafts appear at 46 F.R.D. 161 (1969) and 51 F.R.D. 315 (1971). In addition, there were drafts that were not formally published. The draft adopted and promulgated by the Supreme Court appears at 56 F.R.D. 183 (1972).

[4] Pub. L. No. 93-12, 87 Stat. 9, 93d Cong. 1st Sess.

OVERVIEW

Article I. General Provisions

Rules 101 and 102 state the scope of the Federal Rules of Evidence and their objective "that the truth may be ascertained and proceedings justly determined." The procedural aspects of admission and exclusion are governed by Rule 103, which continues existing law to the effect that error is harmless if it does not affect "substantial rights." Rule 103 also assures that the "plain error" doctrine will be applicable to civil as well as criminal cases and codifies principles concerning objections and proffers. Rule 104 resolves some of the confusion as to how and by whom preliminary fact questions respecting qualifications, competency, admissibility, and the like are to be determined. It provides that the judge ordinarily will make the determination, and that his reception of materials in connection with such determination will be largely unrestrained by the rules of evidence. Rule 105 codifies the "multiple admissibility" rule. A party's right to prevent out-of-context portions of writings and recordings is restated with clarifications in Rule 106, which provides that related materials must be presented contemporaneously with the part, in appropriate circumstances.

One of the rules of the Supreme Court's version was deleted from the final enactment. It specified that the trial judge might sum up and comment on the weight of the evidence for the benefit of the jury, provided that he did so fairly. The purpose of the deletion was not to remove this power, which existing federal case law conferred[5] (in contradistinction to many states[6]), but merely, it would seem, to avoid encouraging its liberal use, and to avoid placing in the evidence rules a provision that was deemed procedural.[7] The deletion is unfortunate, however, because judges under previous law have been reluctant to exercise this power.[8] With the increased admissibility accomplished throughout these new rules [9] and

---

[5] See Vicksburg & M. RR. v. Putnam, 118 U.S. 545 (1886).

[6] See Wright, *The Invasion of the Jury: Temperature of the War*, 27 TEMPLE L. Q. 137 (1973).

[7] See Report, House Judiciary Committee, to accompany H.R. 5463, Rep. No. 93-650, 93d Cong. 1st Sess., Nov. 15, 1973, at Rule 105, stating that the status quo should be preserved, and reserving the merits for future consideration. A committee print dated June 28, 1973, provides further insight into the reasoning of the House Criminal Justice subcommittee proposing the deletion to the Judiciary Committee.

[8] See Kalven & Zeisel, THE AMERICAN JURY 417-25 (1966).

[9] See, e.g., Article VI, cutting down on witness incompetencies; Article VII, opening the door wider to opinion and expert testimony; Article VIII, eroding the hearsay rule; Article IX, expanding the list of self-authenticating documents; and Article X,

the generally high competence of the federal judiciary, this additional tool for guiding the jury's evaluation of evidence could be salutary. Existing law does provide safeguards against this tool's abuse.[10]

In addition, one cannot help but lament that Rule 103 chose not to attempt to spell out in more detail some of the vague operative concepts therein ("substantial rights," "plain error," "timely, specific objection," "offer of proof"), referring us instead to existing case law. For example, Dean Mason Ladd has written an extensive article devoted in large measure to the matters contained in the few lines of Rule 103(a)(1) and (2) (effect of erroneous ruling: objections, offers of proof).[11]

Article II. Judicial Notice

This article consists of one rule, Rule 201. Only "adjudicative facts" are covered. Judicial notice will be taken of them if and only if they are beyond reasonable dispute in that they are generally known in the jurisdiction or easily ascertainable by resort to virtually unimpeachable sources. The procedural effect of judicial notice differs in civil and criminal cases. In civil cases the court is to instruct the jury to accept as conclusive any fact judicially noticed, but in criminal cases, the fact may, but need not, be found, owing to possible conflict with the right to jury trial. The primary impact of the rule is to allow a proposition of fact to be established in ways other than by evidence adduced at trial—by arguments to the court that call on the judge's common knowledge; by documents or books that might be hearsay; or by community word-of-mouth. Of course, the reasonably indisputable criterion must be met.

Rule 201 provides a superb and clear-cut mechanism for handling judicial notice in those areas it covers. It is regrettable that the drafters chose not to provide a similar rational mechanism for handling judicial notice of matters of law.[12]

Article III. Presumptions in Civil Actions and Proceedings

Although earlier versions of the Rules contained provisions covering presumptions in criminal proceedings, the final version speaks

---

providing for the reception of Xerox copies and the like as originals. See also Rules 405 and 608, allowing character proof by opinion.

[10] See Vanderbilt, MINIMUM STANDARDS OF JUDICIAL ADMINISTRATION 224-29 (1949).

[11] *Objections, Motions, and Foundation Testimony,* 43 CORNELL L. Q. 543 (1958).

[12] See, e.g., CAL. EVID. CODE § 452.

only to civil cases.[13] It provides, in Rule 301, that the effect of any presumption is to place the burden of going forward to rebut the presumption on the party opposing it. The burden of persuasion is not placed on that party, as it was under the draft promulgated by the Supreme Court. The effect has been to lighten substantially the force of a presumption. It is unclear just what continuing effect, if any, the presumption is to have if the party opposing the presumption does go forward as contemplated by the rule.

It should be noted that particular presumptions are not established by the Rules. They only prescribe the effect of a presumption found elsewhere in the law.[14]

Pursuant to considerations arising out of *Erie R. Co. v. Tompkins,*[15] the Rules defer to state law concerning the effect of presumptions regarding elements of issues governed by state substantive law.

It is unfortunate that the position of the Supreme Court draft was reversed on the effect of presumptions, since it answered many of the questions left open by the final draft (particularly those relating to the effect of counter-evidence), and gave greater force to the policies that underlie the creation of presumptions.[16] In addition, the deletion of criminal presumptions leaves the difficult subject of such presumptions its current uncertain limbo, at least until Congress gets around to enacting pending bill S.1, which promises to cover it (but only partly).[17]

Article IV. Relevancy and Its Limits

Rule 401 expansively defines relevant evidence as any evidence having "any tendency to make the existence of a fact that is of consequence [18] to the determination of the action more probable or less probable" to any degree than it appeared before. However,

---

[13] Criminal presumptions presumably are to be dealt with in pending Senate bill S. 1, the revision of the federal criminal code.

[14] Compare CAL. EVID. CODE §§ 620-69.

[15] 304 U.S. 64 (1938).

[16] See Testimony, P. Rothstein, Hearings on H.R. 5463, Rules of Evidence, Senate Judiciary Committee, 93d Cong., 2d Sess., June 4-5, 1974, p. 267.

[17] As of the date of this writing, April 15, 1975, hearings are largely completed on S.1 in the Senate, and the bill is about to move from subcommittee to full Judiciary Committee. The House, however, has not yet begun hearings. The coverage of criminal presumptions in S. 1 is not as comprehensive as in the Supreme Court draft of the Federal Rules of Evidence.

[18] "Of consequence" replaces the concept of "materiality," but amounts to the same thing. See Advisory Committee Notes to Rule 401, published with the Supreme Court draft, 56 F.R.D. 183 (1972). For an inconsistency injected by Congress, see the use of the word "material" in Rules 803(24) and 804(b)(5).

while relevance is a prerequisite to admissibility, relevant evidence is not necessarily admissible, and that, in a sense, is what much of the remainder of the Federal Rules of Evidence is about. A large portion of Article IV sets up rules excluding relevant evidence where relevance is regarded as low in comparison with countervailing factors or policies. Article V allows exclusion of evidence, usually no matter how relevant, in the name of some higher objective embodied by a privilege. Article VI in part recognizes at least some incompetencies that have little to do with relevance. And Articles VIII (hearsay), IX (authentication and identification), and X (best evidence) set up safeguards against infirmities in evidence that at least appears relevant.

Rule 402 acknowledges that some relevant evidence may be excepted from admissibility by statute, rule prescribed pursuant to statute, or constitutional principle. Rule 403 formulates the court's broad inherent power to exclude relevant evidence when its probative value is outweighed by other considerations such as prejudice, confusion, and waste of time. Unfair surprise is eliminated as such a consideration owing to the availability (at least in civil cases) of discovery and the possibility of a continuance. Rule 403 thus provides a general guide and safeguard not only for situations not covered by specific rules, but also for all evidence, unless a contrary intention is manifest. Thus, Rule 403 (as a kind of "great override") should be borne in mind in considering all the rules.

Some particular problems of circumstantial evidence are covered in Rules 404–411, which in a sense are particularized judgments about how the Rule 403 considerations (together with certain other policy considerations) must be applied to exclude certain categories of evidence (but not mandating *admission* in any case). Rules 404 and 405, dealing with character evidence, substantially retain existing law as to the admission of character traits as circumstantial evidence but provide that proof of an admissible character trait shall be based on the testimony of lay or expert witnesses about their opinion of the person in question's character or his reputation for such character. Many federal and state courts have excluded opinion. Proof by showing specific instances of conduct has generally been disapproved, as it is here. Another innovation is the allowance of the question, addressed to a good character witness, "Did you know" of past derelictions, as well as the traditional question "Have you heard."

Rule 406 regulates the admission of evidence of human habit

or practice used to show the probability that a person or entity acted in conformity therewith. It attempts to remove certain qualifications which under existing law in some state and federal courts have impeded such admission, i.e., a corroboration requirement or a requirement that there be no eyewitness. However, the language of the rule states only that *relevance,* rather than *admissibility,* does not depend on these conditions, and leaves open the possibility that the evidence, though relevant, may be excluded by consideration of these conditions under the balancing process under Rule 403.

Rules 404–406 are a bit cryptic in their brevity, and the division of material amongst them and amongst the subdivisions thereof, could perhaps have been done in a less confusing way. Also, a nonexistent distinction is drawn in Rule 404 (b) between adducing wrongs to show conduct in conformity with character and adducing them to show "motive, . . . intent, . . . plan, . . . identity, or absence of mistake or accident." In addition, some guidance in distinguishing "character" from "habit" or "routine practice" would have been useful.

Rules 407–411 essentially codify (with some adjustments) traditional exclusionary rules and their exceptions relating to certain so-called implied admissions of a party, assuming any hearsay hurdle (Article VIII) is overcome, which would normally be the case. Rule 407 deals with evidence of remedial measures taken after an alleged dereliction, such as repairs, safety precautions, change of rules or practices, discharge of employees, etc. Rules 408 and 409 cover the ground dealt with by the traditional rule regarding evidence of settlement matters and the like. Rule 410 conditions the use of certain criminal pleas or withdrawn pleas, and statements in connection therewith, carrying over the philosophy encouraging compromise found in Rule 408. Rule 411 relates to proof suggesting insurance coverage. (Such evidence technically may or may not be an implied admission, but in any case it is covered at this point by the Rules.) The kinds of evidence covered by these rules are banned because of doubts as to the trier's ability to appreciate that the probative value is low, the trier's propensity to direct these kinds of evidence other than to the merits, and/or an extrinsic policy to encourage the conduct that would be used as evidence.

One noteworthy feature of Rule 408 is that, unlike many decisions, it extends the ban to conduct or statements made during the compromise negotiations. This operates regardless of whether any special word form was used in the discussion to preserve the immunity, such as stating that the matter is "hypothetical," "conditional," or without prejudice.

Article V. Privileges

The Supreme Court version of the Rules specified nine privileges, each in a separate rule, which were to govern uniformly in all federal cases. These were contained in Article V, together with several rules of general applicability to all the privileges. The final congressional version provides instead only one rule, which states that a federal court shall refer to state law (which state?) in determining the existence and scope of privileges in civil cases where an item of proof tends to support or defeat an element of a claim or defense for which state law supplies the rule of decision. In all other instances the courts are referred to the "principles of the common law as they may be interpreted by the Courts of the United States in the light of reason and experience." This deference to both state and common law will preserve many of the problems in the present law concerning privileges, and will create additional ones. It runs counter to the purposes of a code of evidence and side-steps most of the hard issues in privilege law. The present author has set forth elsewhere his views on this rule and the analogous provision concerning witness competency (Rule 601).[19]

Rule 501 makes exception for statutes, constitutional law, or authorized federal court rules that run counter to it.

Article VI. Witnesses

Article VI divides naturally into three parts. Rules 601–606 deal with the competency of witnesses. Rules 607–610 deal with their credibility. And Rules 611–615 cover a miscellany of mechanical matters respecting the examination and cross-examination of witnesses and related principles.

Rule 601 as promulgated by the Supreme Court eliminated the use in federal proceedings of all grounds of witness incompetency not specifically recognized in Rules 602–606. The rule as enacted, however, provides an exception. In civil cases, state law shall determine competency with respect to an element of a claim or defense as to which state law supplies the rule of decision. This provision parallels the privilege provision, and the objections to it are similar.

---

[19] At 62 GEO. L. J. 125 (1973) and 24 FEDERATION OF INSURANCE COUNSEL QUARTERLY 54 (1974).

It should be noted that unlike the privilege rule, Rule 601 provides that Rules 602–606 rather than a federal common law govern in instances where the court is not to refer to state evidence law.

Rule 607 changes traditional law by allowing a party to impeach his own witness as freely as any other witness. However, an accident of the draftsmanship of Rules 608 (b) and 609 (rules providing for attacks on credibility character through convictions and other wrongdoing) has confined attacks under those rules to attacks made during cross-examination, which raises doubts about use against one's own witness, unless impeachment examination of one's own witness can be regarded as cross-examination rather than direct examination. Perhaps Rule 614 could be invoked to help. It provides that the judge may, in his discretion, call a witness, and that all parties may then *cross-examine* the witness. This drafting problem with Rules 608 (b) and 609 may also preclude their use against an absent declarant whose hearsay statement comes in pursuant to an exception to or other exemption from the hearsay rule, despite Rule 806 which provides that a declarant may be impeached as if he were a witness.

The Rules generally require that the propensity for truthfulness or untruthfulness be shown only by reputation or opinion evidence. Rules 608 (b) and 609 contain exceptions which allow specific instance evidence, i.e., misconduct (608 (b)) and certain criminal convictions (609).

The allowance of opinion evidence is somewhat of an innovation and raises questions as to how far it will be permitted to go. What about opinions of polygraph operators, F.B.I. agents who have interviewed the witness or the accused, or a psychiatrist who has examined the witness or the accused, or has observed him from the courtroom spectators' gallery as in the Alger Hiss trial?

The Court version of Rule 609 allowed impeachment of the witness with conviction of any felony as well as any crime involving dishonesty or false statement. The enacted rule, however, makes the admission of a felony conviction dependent upon the court's determination that its probative value outweighs its prejudicial effect upon the "defendant." Does this use of the word "defendant" treat the two sides of the lawsuit unequally? Were the drafters thinking only of criminal cases? And were they thinking only of cases where the witness *is* the criminal defendant? Did they contemplate that a "defendant" could be prejudiced by an attack on his witness' character? These things remain unresolved, and the legislative history of the rules will play a large role in their determination.

The "American" or restrictive view of the permissible scope of cross-examination, subscribed to by a majority of the states and most federal courts under existing law, is adopted by Rule 611, in contrast to the wide-open or "English" view found in the Supreme Court's version. Discretion to allow inquiry into additional matters remains in the court. And, of course, impeachment matters are not affected by the rule.

Rule 613 changes conventional law as to the foundation that must be laid before a former statement of a witness can be used. No longer must the statement, if written, be shown to the witness. The rule applies the same foundation requirements to written statements as to oral ones. The foundation required is essentially that formerly required for oral statements except that the opportunity for the witness to confront the statement need not come during cross-examination or even before the introduction of the statement, so long as he is eventually recalled to have the opportunity. This enables several mendacious witnesses to be examined before the "cat is out of the bag."

Article VII. Opinions and Expert Testimony

Rule 701 relaxes the rule of some traditional restrictive decisions holding that lay witnesses cannot express opinions, conclusions, or inferences unless articulation of more primary component facts is so impossible or impracticable that they must necessarily be expressed as a shorthand "collective fact." The new standard is that such opinions, etc., are allowed if they are "helpful" and rationally based on perception.

As to expert witnesses, Rule 702 follows a liberal line of decisions, requiring that the testimony be of assistance to the trier of fact, not that the area testified to be beyond lay comprehension. Furthermore, a witness may qualify as an expert even if his expertise is based solely on "knowledge," "skill," "experience," or "training" rather than on formal education.

Under Rule 703, the "facts or data" upon which the expert bases his opinion can be presented to him in ways other than through the traditional open court hypothetical question. The rule seems to allow as a basis material put to the expert beforehand (perhaps in an out-of-court hypothetical), personal observation, and material the expert has heard from the witnesses during the trial.

(But note the possible conflict with Rule 615, sequestering witnesses on request). The facts and data relied upon by the expert need not be admitted or even admissible into evidence if they are of a type "reasonably relied upon by experts in the particular field." While many courts have purported to apply a stricter standard demanding that the facts and data be of an admissible nature or actually admitted, such a standard is impossible to enforce because an expert necessarily relies on much inadmissible evidence, e.g., textbooks, studies, consultations with others, things his teachers and patients have told him, medical reports, histories and charts, x-rays, reports, copies, etc., much of which is hearsay or unauthenticated or in violation of the best-evidence rule.

The underlying facts and data (including, presumably, the material which would normally be in a hypothetical, and studies, consultations, reasons, etc.) need not be disclosed on direct examination of the expert unless the court requires it (Rule 705), although failure to do so may be tactically unwise in many cases.

It is unclear under the rules whether inadmissible information that forms an expert's basis can *itself* be recounted (either on direct or in response to cross-examination as to basis), or whether the rules merely mean to license an *opinion* based thereon.

Rule 704, in accord with the Rules' expanded reception of opinions, both lay and expert, when helpful to the trier of fact, specifically refuses to apply the traditional ban against opinions as to "an ultimate issue." Rules 403, 701, and 702 prohibit opinions that are not "helpful" or "of assistance" or are a waste of time, prejudicial, misleading, or confusing, and thus provide some assurance against admission of opinions that add little to what the jury can do without them, or which merely exhort the jury to award the decision to a particular party. These concepts may indeed result in a ban on opinions on ultimate issues in many instances.

The court appointment of experts is now regulated by Rule 706.

The tendency of the Rules to be guidelines only, with large measures of judicial discretion, and to rely on the inherent wisdom and restraint of federal trial and appellate judges, is nowhere more apparent than in Article VII[20] (and also perhaps in Rule 403). It

---

[20] For example, were it not for an Advisory Committee note specifically addressed to accident reconstruction experts here and in the analogous portion of the California Evidence Code (see Note, Supreme Court draft, Rule 703, and Comment, Cal. Law

cannot be gainsaid that the attempt of Article VII to bring us into the twentieth century and to permit courts to receive the benefits of many of today's specialized areas of knowledge by lowering tradi-tional barriers to expert testimony is a worthy one. But the various states, which on a wholesale basis will begin considering these rules for adoption, should want to examine individually whether the par-ticular courts, both high and low, that will be administering the rules have the competence to administer them wisely, or whether more specificity is desirable. It is an interesting sidelight, however, that in all the deliberations on these rules, Congress never once sug-gested that Article VII should be changed in any way.

It should be noted that to the extent the rules leave latitude to trial and appellate judges, they will invite appeals (heightened by the appeal-mindedness the new knowledge promoted by these rules can be expected to stimulate), case development, re-invigoration of existing case law, unpredictability, inability to advise and plan with certainty, a lack of uniformity amongst circuits, time-consuming legal research beyond the two covers of the rules themselves, and enmity by dissatisfied litigants against judges rather than against the inevitable law. To this extent, then, the hoped-for benefits of codifi-cation will not be realized.

This is not to say the Rules are bad. In fact, in this author's opinion, they have successfully struck the balance between undue rigidity and unguided flexibility, even in Article VII, in view of the competence of the judiciary that will be administering them. The point is, one should not have unrealistic expectations concerning the benefits of codification. There will be benefits; but the theoreti-cal goals will not be attained 100 percent.

Rev. Comm., Recommendation Proposing an Evidence Code 148-50 (1965)), there would be nothing to prevent a court from admitting a so-called accidentologist's conclusion that a designated party "was at fault" formulated on the basis solely of interviews with bystanders. He might persuade some court that is so minded to hold that all the criteria of the rules are met: "specialized knowledge," "helpful" or "of assistance," based on material usually (and therefore reasonably) relied on by other accidentol-ogists, couched in terms allowed by the abolition of the ultimate issues rule. While there is a note to prevent it in this case (courts have been known to disregard notes), the problem goes beyond accidentologists to a multitude of today's fields of expertise, real and pretended. Legal investigators, sociologists, psychologists, or former employees of regulatory agencies or businesses may have specialized knowledge in certain areas, such as the consumer behavior of poor people in credit practice cases, employment practices or attitudes in discrimination cases, competitive effects in antitrust cases, etc. Underlying data may have come from totally inadequate samplings, or adequate samplings, or other suspect or non-suspect sources. The problem will be to differ-entiate the good from the bad, and the Rules do not help much without resort to other principles of law, which may or may not be consulted, at least in the early years.

Article VIII. Hearsay

Rule 801 provides the definitional framework for the hearsay rules. Hearsay is confined to "statements." Conduct is equivalent to a statement only if it is assertive, i.e., intended as a substitute for words, contrary to some decisions that recognize that nonassertive conduct offered in certain situations can present credibility problems akin to direct expressions and should be regarded as implied hearsay statements. ("Assertive" conduct would be, e.g., nodding agreement or pointing in answer to a question; "nonassertive" conduct presenting hearsay-type credibility problems would be X chasing Y at a crime scene, offered to support the proposition that Y committed the crime.)

There is a hiatus in the rule. The rule does not tell us how to handle a situation where previous law might have recognized that one statement is in reality being offered as tantamount to another statement (implied from the first statement). For example, X is heard saying to Y at the scene of the crime, "You no good dog," and this statement is offered to help show that Y committed the crime. Hearsay is only hearsay if the statement is offered for its truth (see Rule 801 (c)), which it is not here. But if the real statement here is the implied statement by X that "You did it, Y, you dirty dog," then it is being offered for its truth. While Rule 801 tells us when nonverbal conduct can give rise to an implied hearsay statement, it does not tell us when words can, or which of the two quoted statements above (the expressed one or the implied one) must be offered for its truth before we have hearsay.

The prior statement of a witness who is testifying is considered hearsay under the general portion of the rule, but 801 (d) specifies that under certain conditions, prior statements by witnesses and admissions of party opponents or agents are given "non-hearsay" status. This permitting of prior statements for more than impeachment purposes has not been a generally followed position. The exemption for admissions is traditional, although the terminology usually used has been "exception to the hearsay rule" rather than "non-hearsay."

Aside from this, the Rules follow the common law approach to hearsay, generally excluding it but making exceptions. The exceptions, also drawn from the common law, are collected under two rules. Rule 803 codifies the exceptions for which availability of the declarant is immaterial. Rule 804 codifies the exceptions for which unavailability is a condition of admissibility. Both of these rules conclude with a "catchall" provision for hearsay statements not within one of the specified exceptions but having "equivalent circumstantial guarantees of trustworthiness" if the evidence is needed and notice is given. The intent is to encourage development of the law in this area while conserving past values and experience as a guide. The specifically codified exceptions also manifest an attitude favoring admissibility, codifying, where there was a choice, the more liberal decisions and statutes.

Some of the areas in which Rule 803 differs from traditional law are the following: An exception for present sense impression is included (803 (1)). Rule 803 (4), "statements for purposes of medical diagnosis or treatment," expands the traditional exception to include statements to medical personnel other than doctors and statements made by other persons than the patient if germane to the patient's diagnosis or treatment. Rule 803 (5), "recorded recollection," adopts a middle ground between requiring complete lack of memory and allowing the evidence regardless of the state of memory. Rule 803 (6), "records of regularly conducted activity," broadens the traditional business-records exception as to the type of organization that qualifies and the kind of thing that may be reported. Rule 803 (7) recognizes an exception for the absence of entries kept in accordance with 803(6). Rules 803(17) and (18), various publications, go beyond most accepted decisions.

In Rule 804 (a) a uniform definition of "unavailability" is adopted for all applicable hearsay exceptions. Under traditional law, the definition often varied with the exception.

The "former testimony" exception in the Rules requires stricter identity of parties than did the Court version but liberalizes the requirement as found in many decisions. The exception is codified in 804(b)(1). The "dying declaration" exception as expressed in 804(b)(2) is broader than at common law in that it applies to other types of cases in addition to criminal homicide prosecutions, and the declarant need not actually die but need only believe he is about to die. Rule 804(b)(3), "statements against interest," also changes traditional law by including in the exception statements against penal interest. The exception is limited by the requirement of clear corroboration as a condition of admitting a statement of a third party exculpating the accused. An exception for statements of "recent perception" was eliminated from the final version of the Rules.

Article IX. Authentication and Identification

This article provides uniform methods for authenticating and identifying documents and objects. Rule 902 greatly expands the list of documents which are self-authenticating, that is, documents to which a rebuttable presumption of genuineness attaches.

Article X. Contents of Writings, Recordings, and Photographs

This article is the "best evidence" or "original documents" rule. Rule 1001 spells out the applicability of Article X to documents and modern analogues of documents, including electronic and mechanical picture and data processes. The principal reforms are a somewhat expanded definition of an "original" document and the creation of a category between "originals" and "copies" called "duplicates," ordinarily receivable on a par with originals. This includes Xeroxes. The Rules recognize no degrees of preference as to secondary evidence when the "original" is unavailable.

Article XI. Miscellaneous Rules

This article specifies in which courts and to which actions and proceedings the Rules apply. Rule 1102 provides for amendment of the Rules in compliance with the procedures set forth in new 28 U.S.C. 2076.

MOTIFS

We have already commented above on what seems to be a "trust the judge" attitude in the Rules. It should also be apparent that the Rules in addition "trust the jury." They admit more evidence than traditionally has been allowed and rely on the jury to evaluate it properly with the help of the judge and the attorneys. This implies a "trust of lawyers" as well, because it assumes parties will be represented by competent counsel who can be depended upon to effectively point out strengths and weaknesses in evidence. The competence of the particular bar to be governed by the Rules is an important consideration.

The Rules also have implications for investigation burdens and the allocation of advantage between prosecution and defense in criminal cases, and concerning the freedom of appellate courts, all of which are commented on elsewhere.[21] Suffice it to say here that

---

[21] Rothstein, *Some Themes in the Proposed Federal Rules of Evidence*, 33 FEDERAL BAR JOURNAL 21 (1974).

certain expenses formerly placed on the proponent of evidence are now shifted to the opponent. Whether this will more often work for or against the litigant of small means and whether some change in methods of awarding costs or supporting indigent litigants is required remain to be seen. Concerning relative advantage in criminal cases, the prosecution gains from the generally increased admissibility in those cases where the defense hopes to rely on the prosecution's inability to meet its burden. Greater admissibility means it is easier to "prove beyond a reasonable doubt." The prosecution also has a reasonably favorable tool in several of the rules, including, among others, the rule granting substantive admissibility to prior witness statements, e.g., statements made to the grand jury (Rule 801 (d)(1)(A)), and the rule excluding third-party confessions excusing the accused unless clearly corroborated (Rule 804(b)(3)). (Under many decisions, however, third-party confessions were totally inadmissible, which was even more favorable to the prosecution.) At the same time, the prosecution is allowed to introduce them when they *inculpate,* without such restriction, despite doubts under existing law.

On the other hand, certain rules clearly disfavor the prosecution. For example, Rule 801(d)(1)(C), admitting a witness's prior out-of-court identification statements in accord with a growing trend, has been deleted by Congress. And, while the prosecution has been given a reasonably favorable rule on impeachment by convictions, this rule (609) could have been even more favorable. Whether Rule 609 (and Rule 608, broadening, for impeachment, the use of character-opinion and misconduct that is not a conviction) will be utilized more often *by* or *against* the prosecution, who frequently must rely on some disreputable witnesses, is an open question. The same duality inheres in the similar broadening of *substantive* character evidence to include opinion evidence (Rule 405).

Thus, the Rules promise to usher in an era which, while somewhat different from the old, is still recognizable. The Rules' more extravagant promises of complete simplicity, certainty, and uniformity, will not be realized; but neither will fears of "uneven-handedness." All told, with evolution over time, the Rules should provide a discernible improvement in the operation of federal courts.

Rules of Evidence for United States Courts and Magistrates

Text of the Rules with comment derived from the Notes of the Advisory Committee on Rules of Evidence; House Report (Judiciary Committee) No. 93–650; Senate Report (Judiciary Committee) No. 93–1277; and House Conference Report No. 93–1597.

ARTICLE I. GENERAL PROVISIONS

Rule 101. Scope

These rules govern proceedings in the courts of the United States and before United States magistrates, to the extent and with the exceptions stated in rule 1101.

COMMENT: Rule 101 is as drafted by the Advisory Committee on Rules of Evidence and specifies courts, proceedings, questions, and stages of proceedings to which the rules apply in whole or in part. See Rule 1101.

Rule 102. Purpose and Construction

These rules shall be construed to secure fairness in administration, elimination of unjustifiable expense and delay, and promotion of growth and development of the law of evidence to the end that the truth may be ascertained and proceedings justly determined.

COMMENT: Rule 102 is similar to FED. R. CRIM. P. 2; FED. R. CIV. P. 1; CAL. EVIDENCE CODE § 2; and N. J. EVIDENCE Rule 5. The rule as drafted by the Advisory Committee was adopted verbatim by the Congress.

Rule 103. Rulings on Evidence

(a) **Effect of erroneous ruling.** Error may not be predicated upon a ruling which admits or excludes evidence unless a substantial right of the party is affected, and

(1) **Objection.** In case the ruling is one admitting evidence, a timely objection or motion to strike appears of record, stating the specific ground of objection, if the specific ground was not apparent from the context; or

(2) **Offer of proof.** In case the ruling is one excluding evidence, the substance of the evidence was made known to the court by offer or was apparent from the context within which questions were asked.

(b) **Record of offer and ruling.** The court may add any other or further statement which shows the character of the evidence, the form in which it was offered, the objection made, and the ruling thereon. It may direct the making of an offer in question and answer form.

(c) **Hearing of jury.** In jury cases, proceedings shall be conducted, to the extent practicable, so as to prevent inadmissible evidence from being suggested to the jury by any means, such as making statements or offers of proof or asking questions in the hearing of the jury.

(d) **Plain error.** Nothing in this rule precludes taking notice of plain errors affecting substantial rights although they were not brought to the attention of the court.

COMMENT: No substantive change in this rule was made by the Congress; it is as adopted by the Advisory Committee. Therefore the following Advisory Committee note remains pertinent:

"**Subdivision (a)** states the law as generally accepted today. Rulings on evidence cannot be assigned as error unless (1) a substantial right is affected, and (2) the nature of the error was called to the attention of the judge, so as to alert him to the proper course of action and enable opposing counsel to take proper corrective measures. The objection and the offer of proof are the techniques for accomplishing these objectives. For similar provisions see Uniform Rules 4 and 5; California Evidence Code §§ 353 and 354; Kansas Code of Civil Procedure §§ 60–404 and 60–405. The status of constitutional error as harmless or not is treated in Chapman v. California, 386 U.S. 18, 87 S.Ct. 824, 17 L.Ed.2d 705 (1967), reh. denied *id.* 987, 87 S.Ct. 1238, 18 L.Ed.2d 241.

"**Subdivision (b).** The first sentence is the third sentence of Rule 43 (c) of the Federal Rules of Civil Procedure virtually verbatim. Its purpose is to reproduce for an appellate court, insofar as possible, a true reflection of what occurred in the trial court. The second sentence is in part derived from the final sentence of Rule 43 (c). It is designed to resolve doubts as to what testimony the witness would have in fact given, and, in nonjury cases, to provide the appellate court with material for a possible final disposition of the case in the event of reversal of a ruling which excluded evidence. See 5 Moore's Federal Practice 43.11 (2d ed. 1968). Application is made discretionary in view of the practical impossibility of formulating a satisfactory rule in mandatory terms.

"**Subdivision (c).** This subdivision proceeds on the supposition that a ruling which excludes evidence in a jury case is likely to be a pointless procedure if the excluded evidence nevertheless comes to the attention of the jury. Bruton v. United States, 389 U.S. 818, 88 S.Ct. 126, 19 L.Ed.2d 70 (1968). Rule 43 (c) of the Federal Rules of Civil Procedure provides: 'The court may require the offer to be made out of the hearing of the jury.' In re McConnell, 370 U.S. 230, 82 S.Ct. 1288, 8 L.Ed.2d 434 (1962), left some doubt whether questions on which an offer is based must first be asked in the presence of the jury. The subdivision answers in the negative. The judge can foreclose a particular line of testimony and counsel can protect his record without a series of questions before the jury, designed at best to waste time and at worst 'to waft into the jury box' the very matter sought to be excluded.

"**Subdivision (d).** This wording of the plain error principle is from Rule 52 (b) of the Federal Rules of Criminal Procedure. While judicial unwillingness to be constricted by mechanical breakdowns of the adversary system has been more pronounced in criminal cases, there is no scarcity of decisions to the same effect in civil cases. In general, see Campbell, Extent to Which Courts of Review Will Consider Questions Not Properly Raised and Preserved, 7 Wis. L. Rev. 91, 160 (1932) ; Vestal, Sua Sponte Consideration in Appellate Review, 27 Fordham L. Rev. 477 (1958–59) ; 64 Harv. L. Rev. 652 (1951). In the nature of things the application of the plain error rule will be more likely with respect to the admission of evidence than to exclusion since failure to comply with normal requirements of offers of proof is likely to produce a record which simply does not disclose the error."

Rule 104. Preliminary Questions

(a) **Questions of admissibility generally.** Preliminary questions concerning the qualification of a person to be a witness, the existence of a privilege, or the admissibility of evidence shall be determined by the court, subject to the provisions of subdivision (b). In making its determination it is not bound by the rules of evidence except those with respect to privileges.

(b) **Relevancy conditioned on fact.** When the relevancy of evidence depends upon the fulfillment of a condition of fact, the court shall admit it upon, or subject to, the introduction of evidence sufficient to support a finding of the fulfillment of the condition.

(c) **Hearing of jury.** Hearings on the admissibility of confessions shall in all cases be conducted out of the hearing of the jury. Hearings on other preliminary matters shall be so conducted when the interests of justice require or, when an accused is a witness, if he so requests.

(d) **Testimony by accused.** The accused does not, by testifying upon a preliminary matter, subject himself to cross-examination as to other issues in the case.

(e) **Weight and credibility.** This rule does not limit the right of a party to introduce before the jury evidence relevant to weight or credibility.

COMMENT: This rule as enacted by Congress is substantially the same as that promulgated by the Supreme Court, except that subdivision (c) was amended to provide for preliminary hearings outside of the hearing of a jury "when an accused is a witness, if he so requests." The House Committee on the Judiciary, in HOUSE REPORT NO. 93–650, recognized that in some cases duplication of evidence would occur and that the procedure could be subject to abuse, but nevertheless believed "that a proper regard for the right of an accused not to testify generally in the case dictates that he be given an option to testify out of the presence of the jury on preliminary matters." The Committee also noted that it construed the second sentence of subdivision (c) as applying to civil actions and proceedings as well as to criminal cases, and "on this assumption left the sentence unamended."

In SENATE REPORT NO. 93–1277, the Senate Committee on the Judiciary commented on subdivision (d), even though that subdivision was left undisturbed. That comment reads as follows:

"Under Rule 104 (c) the hearing on a preliminary matter may at times be conducted in front of the jury. Should an accused testify in such a hearing, waiving his privilege against self-incrimination as to the preliminary issue, Rule 104 (d) provides that he will not generally be subject to cross-examination as to any other issue. This rule is not, however, intended to immunize the accused from cross-examination where, in testifying about a preliminary issue, he injects other issues into the hearing. If he could not be cross-examined about any issues gratuitously raised by him beyond the scope of the preliminary matters, injustice might result. Accordingly, in order to prevent any such unjust result, the committee intends the rule to be construed to provide that the accused may subject himself to cross-examination as to issues raised by his own testimony upon a preliminary matter before a jury."

The Advisory Committee in its note to subdivision (a) explains that the applicability of a particular rule of evidence often depends on the existence of a condition. In each instance the admissibility of evidence will turn upon the answer to the question of the existence of the condition. Accepted practice, incorporated in the rule, places on the judge the responsibility for these determinations. [McCORMICK ON EVIDENCE § 53; MORGAN, BASIC PROBLEMS OF EVIDENCE 45–50(1962).]

Often rulings on evidence call not only for a determination of fact but also for an evaluation in terms of a legally set standard. Thus, the subdivision refers to preliminary requirements generally by the broad term "questions," without attempted specification. While subdivision (a) is of general application, it must be read as subject to the special provisions for "conditional relevancy" in subdivision (b) and those for confessions in subdivision (d). In determining matters of fact, the judge of necessity receives evidence pro and con on the issue, but the rule provides that the rules of evidence in general do not apply to this process.

The Advisory Committee note to subdivision (b) points out that if preliminary questions of conditional relevancy were determined solely by the judge, as provided in subdivision (a), the functioning of the jury as a trier of fact would be greatly restricted and in some cases virtually destroyed. Accepted treatment, as provided in the rule, is consistent with that given questions of fact generally. The judge makes a preliminary determination of whether the foundation evidence is sufficient to support a finding of the fulfillment of the condition. If so, the item is admitted. If after all the evidence on the issue is in, pro and con, the jury could reasonably conclude that fulfillment of the condition is not established, the issue is for the jury. If the evidence is not such as to allow a finding, the judge withdraws the matter from the jury's consideration. The order of proof here is subject to the control of the judge.

The Advisory Committee note to subdivision (c) emphasizes that under *Jackson* v. *Denno*, 378 U.S. 368 (1964), preliminary hearings on the admissibility of confessions must be conducted outside the presence of the jury.

The Committee also observes that not infrequently the same evidence relevant to the issue of establishment of fulfillment of a condition precedent to admissibility is also relevant to weight and credibility, and time is saved by taking foundation proof in the presence of the jury. Much evidence on preliminary questions, though not relevant to jury issues, may be heard by the jury with no adverse effect. A great deal, according to the Committee, must be left to the discretion of the court, which will act as the interests of justice require.

With respect to subdivision (d) the Committee declares that the limitation upon cross-examination is designed to encourage participation by the accused in the determination of preliminary matters. Under the rule he may testify concerning such matters without exposing himself to cross-examination generally.

Subdivision (e) is, the Advisory Committee points out, similar to CAL. EVIDENCE CODE § 406; KANS. CODE CIVIL P. § 60–408; and N.J. EVIDENCE Rule 8 (1).

Rule 105. Limited Admissibility

When evidence which is admissible as to one party or for one purpose but not admissible as to another party or for another purpose is admitted, the court, upon request, shall restrict the evidence to its proper scope and instruct the jury accordingly.

COMMENT: The rules as submitted by the Supreme Court contained a Rule 105 that would have permitted the judge to sum up and comment on the evidence. The House struck the rule, "intending that its action be understood as reflecting no conclusion as to the merits of the proposed rule and that the subject should be left for separate considera- tion at another time." The Senate accepted the House action "with the understanding that the present federal practice, taken from the common law, of the trial judge's discretionary authority to comment on and sum- marize the evidence is left undisturbed."

Rule 105 on limited admissibility is identical to the limited admissi- bility rule submitted as Rule 106 by the Supreme Court. However, the House Committee on the Judiciary observed that it understood the rule as adopted as not affecting "the authority of a court to order a severence in a multi-defendant case."

The Advisory Committee note on this rule stresses the close rela- tionship between it and Rule 403 (a), which requires exclusion when "probative value is substantially outweighed by the danger of prejudice, of confusion of the issues, or of misleading the jury." The rule recog- nizes the practice of admitting evidence for a limited purpose and in- structing the jury accordingly. The availablity and effectiveness of this practice must be taken into consideration in deciding whether to ex- clude for unfair prejudice under Rule 403.

Similar provisions are found in CAL. EVIDENCE CODE § 355; KANS. CODE CIV. P. § 60–406; and N.J. EVIDENCE Rule 6. The wording of Rule 105 differs from these, however, in that it rules out any implication that limiting or curative instructions are sufficient in all situations.

Rule 106. Remainder of or Related Writings or Recorded Statements

When a writing or recorded statement or part thereof is intro- duced by a party, an adverse party may require him at that time to introduce any other part or any other writing or recorded statement which ought in fairness to be considered contemporaneously with it.

COMMENT: Congress made no change in this rule as it was submitted by the Supreme Court.

The Advisory Committee note on this rule characterizes it as an ex- pression of the rule of completeness. [McCORMICK ON EVIDENCE § 56.] It is, the Committee observes, manifested as to depositions in FED. R. CIV. P. 32 (a) (4), of which the proposed rule is substantially a restatement.

Rule 106 is based on two considerations. The first is the misleading impression created by taking matters out of context. The second is the inadequacy of repair work when delayed to a point later in the trial. It does not in any way circumscribe the right of the adversary to develop the matter on cross-examination or as part of his own case. For practical reasons the rule is limited to writings and recorded statements and does not apply to conversations.

ARTICLE II. JUDICIAL NOTICE

Rule 201. Judicial Notice of Adjudicative Facts

(a) **Scope of rule.** This rule governs only judicial notice of adjudicative facts.

(b) **Kinds of facts.** A judicially noticed fact must be one not subject to reasonable dispute in that it is either (1) generally known within the territorial jurisdiction of the trial court or (2) capable of accurate and ready determination by resort to sources whose accuracy cannot reasonably be questioned.

(c) **When discretionary.** A court may take judicial notice, whether requested or not.

(d) **When mandatory.** A court shall take judicial notice if requested by a party and supplied with the necessary information.

(e) **Opportunity to be heard.** A party is entitled upon timely request to an opportunity to be heard as to the propriety of taking judicial notice and the tenor of the matter noticed. In the absence of prior notification, the request may be made after judicial notice has been taken.

(f) **Time of taking notice.** Judicial notice may be taken at any stage of the proceeding.

(g) **Instructing jury.** In a civil action or proceeding, the court shall instruct the jury to accept as conclusive any fact judicially noticed. In a criminal case, the court shall instruct the jury that it may, but is not required to, accept as conclusive any fact judicially noticed.

COMMENT: With the exception of subdivision (g) Congress adopted this rule as submitted by the Supreme Court.

The Advisory Committee note comments that this is the only evidence rule on the subject of judicial notice and that it deals only with judicial notice of "adjudicative" facts. No rule deals with judicial notice of "legislative" facts. Judicial notice of matters of foreign law is treated in Rule 44.1 of the FEDERAL RULES of CIVIL PROCEDURE and Rule 26.1 of the FEDERAL RULES OF CRIMINAL PROCEDURE. Citing 2 DAVIS, ADMINISTRATIVE LAW TREATISE 353, the Advisory Committee defines adjudicative facts as those "which relate to the parties." Quoting Professor Davis, the Committee notes, "when a court or an agency finds facts concerning the immediate parties—who did what, where, when, how, and with what motive or intent—the court or agency is performing an adjudicative function, and the facts are conveniently called adjudicative facts. . . .

"Stated in other terms, the adjudicative facts are those to which the law is applied in the process of adjudication. They are the facts that normally go to the jury in a jury case. They relate to the parties, their activities, their properties, their businesses."

Commenting on subdivision (b), the Advisory Committee observes that with respect to judicial notice of adjudicative facts, the tradition has been one of caution, requiring that the matter be beyond reasonable controversy. The rule proceeds upon the theory that traditional methods of proof should be dispensed with only in clear cases. The rule is consistent with Uniform Rules 9(1) and (2), which limit judicial notice of facts to those "so universally known that they cannot reasonably be the subject of dispute," those "so generally known or of such common notoriety within the territorial jurisdiction of the court that they cannot reasonably be the subject of dispute," and those "capable of immediate and accurate determination by resort to easily accessible sources of indisputable accuracy." The phrase "propositions of generalized knowledge" found in Uniform Rules 9(1) and (2) is not included in the present rule. It was originally included in the Model Rules to afford some minimum recognition to the right of the judge in his "legislative" capacity to take judicial notice of very limited categories of generalized knowledge. The limitations thus imposed have been discarded in the proposed rules of evidence as undesirable, unworkable, and contrary to existing practice.

With respect to subdivision (c) the Advisory Committee points out that the judge has discretionary authority to take judicial notice, regardless of whether he is so requested by a party. Under subdivision (d), however, the taking of judicial notice is mandatory if a party requests it and the necessary information is supplied. This scheme is believed to reflect existing practice. It is simple and workable. It avoids troublesome distinctions in the many situations in which the process of taking judicial notice is not recognized as such.

Subdivision (e) is prompted by basic considerations of procedural fairness. No formal scheme of giving notice is provided. An adversely affected party may learn in advance that judicial notice is in contemplation either by being served with a copy of a request by another party under subdivision (d) that judicial notice be taken or through an advance indication by the judge. Or he may have no advance notice at all, the likelihood of which is enhanced by the frequent failure to recognize judicial notice as such. And in the absence of advance notice, requests made after the fact could not in fairness be considered untimely.

Subdivision (f) is in accord with the usual view that judicial notice may be taken at any stage of the proceedings, whether in the trial court or on appeal.

As submitted by the Supreme Court, Rule 201 (g) provided that when judicial notice of a fact is taken, the court shall instruct the jury, in both civil and criminal proceedings, to accept that fact as established. The House Committee on the Judiciary was of the view that such a mandatory instruction to a jury in a criminal case would be contrary to the spirit of the sixth-amendment right to a jury trial. Therefore, the Committee adopted the 1969 Advisory Committee draft of this subdivision allowing a mandatory instruction in civil actions and proceedings and a discretionary instruction in criminal cases.

The Advisory Committee note to subdivision (g) asserts that in the rule's relatively narrow area of adjudicative facts, the rule contemplates that there is to be no evidence before the jury in disproof.

Under the rule as submitted to Congress the jury was to be instructed to "accept as established" any facts judicially noticed. Under the rule as amended in Congress the jury is to be instructed to "accept as conclusive" any fact judicially noticed.

ARTICLE III. PRESUMPTIONS IN CIVIL ACTIONS AND PROCEEDINGS

Rule 301. Presumptions in General in Civil Actions and Proceedings

In all civil actions and proceedings not otherwise provided for by Act of Congress or by these rules, a presumption imposes on the party against whom it is directed the burden of going forward with evidence to rebut or meet the presumption, but does not shift to such party the burden of proof in the sense of the risk of nonpersuasion, which remains throughout the trial upon the party on whom it was originally cast.

COMMENT: As submitted by the Supreme Court, presumptions governed by this rule were given the effect of placing upon the opposing party the burden of establishing the nonexistence of the presumed fact, once the party invoking the presumption established the basic facts giving rise to it. As it emerged from the House, the rule provided that a presumption in civil actions and proceedings shifts to the party against whom it is directed the burden of going forward with evidence to meet or rebut it. Even though evidence contradicting the presumption is offered, a presumption is considered sufficient evidence of the presumed fact to be considered by the jury. The Senate amended the rule to provide that a presumption shifts to the party against whom it is directed the burden of going forward with evidence to meet or rebut the presumption, but it does not shift to that party the burden of persuasion on the existence of the presumed fact.

Under the Senate amendment, which was incorporated in the rules of evidence as enacted, a presumption is sufficient to get a party past an adverse party's motion to dismiss made at the end of his case-in-chief. If the adverse party offers no evidence contradicting the presumed fact, the court will instruct the jury that if it finds the basic facts, it may presume the existence of the presumed fact. If the adverse party does offer evidence contradicting the presumed fact, the court cannot instruct the jury that it may presume the existence of the presumed fact from proof of the basic facts. The court may, however, instruct the jury that it may infer the existence of the presumed fact from the proof of the basic facts.

Rule 302. Applicability of State Law in Civil Actions and Proceedings

In civil actions and proceedings, the effect of a presumption respecting a fact which is an element of a claim or defense as to which

State law supplies the rule of decision is determined in accordance with State law.

COMMENT: This rule remains substantially as submitted by the Court. The Advisory Committee note to this section emphasizes the relevance of *Erie Railroad Co.* v. *Tompkins,* 304 U.S. 64 (1938), to questions of burden of proof. The Committee points out, however, that it does not follow that all presumptions in diversity cases are governed by state law. In those burden-of-proof cases in which *Erie* has been applied, the burden-of-proof question had to do with the substantive element of the claim or defense. Application of the state law is called for only when the presumption operates upon such an element. Accordingly, the rule does not apply state law when the presumption operates upon a lesser aspect of the case, i.e., "tactical" presumptions.

Erie, the Committee stresses, applies to any claim or issue having its source in state law, regardless of the basis of federal jurisdiction, and does not apply to a federal claim or issue, even though jurisdiction is based on diversity. Hence, the rule employs, as appropriately descriptive, the phrase "as to which state law supplies the rule of decision."

As submitted by the Supreme Court, Article III contained a rule directed to the issues of when, in criminal cases, a court may submit a presumption to a jury and the type of instruction it should give. This was deleted by the House Committee on the Judiciary since the subject of presumptions in criminal cases is addressed in detail in bills now pending before the Committee to revise the federal criminal code. The Committee will consider this question in the course of its study of the proposed revisions.

ARTICLE IV. RELEVANCY AND ITS LIMITS

Rule 401. Definition of "Relevant Evidence"

"Relevant evidence" means evidence having any tendency to make the existence of any fact that is of consequence to the determination of the action more probable or less probable than it would be without the evidence.

COMMENT: Rule 401 was enacted as submitted by the Supreme Court.

The pertinent Advisory Committee note with respect to this rule comments that relevancy is not an inherent characteristic of any item of evidence but exists only as a relation between an item of evidence and a matter properly provable in the case. The rule summarizes this relationship as a "tendency to make the existence" of the fact to be proved "more probable or less probable." Any more stringent requirement than the expressed standard of probability would be unworkable and unrealistic. Dealing with probability in the language of the rule has the added virtue of avoiding confusion between questions of admissibility and questions of sufficiency of the evidence.

The rule uses the phrase "fact that is of consequence to the determination of the action." The fact to be proved may be ultimate, intermediate, or evidentiary; it matters not, so long as it is of consequence in the determination of the action.

The fact to which the evidence is directed need not be in dispute. A rule limiting admissibility to evidence directed to a controversial point would invite the exclusion of helpful evidence, or at least the raising of endless questions over its admission.

Rule 402. Relevant Evidence Generally Admissible; Irrelevant Evidence Inadmissible

All relevant evidence is admissible, except as otherwise provided by the Constitution of the United States, by Act of Congress, by these rules, or by other rules prescribed by the Supreme Court pursuant to statutory authority. Evidence which is not relevant is not admissible.

COMMENT: Rule 402 as submitted to the Congress contained the phrase "or by other rules adopted by the Supreme Court." To accommodate the view that Congress should not appear to acquiesce in the

Court's judgment that it has authority under the existing Rules Enabling Act to promulgate rules of evidence, the House Committee on the Judiciary amended that phrase to read "or by other rules prescribed by the Supreme Court pursuant to statutory authority" in this and other rules where the reference appears.

Rule 403. Exclusion of Relevant Evidence on Grounds of Prejudice, Confusion, or Waste of Time

Although relevant, evidence may be excluded if its probative value is substantially outweighed by the danger of unfair prejudice, confusion of the issues, or misleading the jury, or by considerations of undue delay, waste of time, or needless presentation of cumulative evidence.

COMMENT: This rule was adopted as submitted by the Supreme Court.

The Advisory Committee note with respect to Rule 403 emphasizes that situations in this area call for balancing the probative value of and need for the evidence against the harm likely to result from its admission. Exclusion for risk of unfair prejudice, confusion of issues, misleading the jury, or waste of time all find ample support in the authorities. However, the Committee explains, waste of time entails no serious likelihood of a miscarriage of justice and hence should be accorded a different treatment.

"Unfair prejudice" within the context of the rule is defined by the Advisory Committee to mean an undue tendency to suggest decision on an improper basis, commonly, though not necessarily, an emotional one.

The Committee note also calls attention to the fact that the rule does not enumerate surprise as a ground for exclusion, in this respect following Wigmore's view of the common law.

With respect to excluding on grounds of unfair prejudice, the Advisory Committee says that consideration should be given to the probable effectiveness or lack of effectiveness of a limiting instruction. The availability of other means of proof may also be an appropriate factor.

Rule 404. Character Evidence Not Admissible to Prove Conduct; Exceptions; Other Crimes

(a) **Character evidence generally.** Evidence of a person's character or a trait of his character is not admissible for the purpose of proving that he acted in conformity therewith on a particular occasion, except:

(1) **Character of accused.** Evidence of a pertinent trait of his character offered by an accused, or by the prosecution to rebut the same;

(2) **Character of victim.** Evidence of a pertinent trait of character of the victim of the crime offered by an accused, or by the prosecution to rebut the same, or evidence of a character trait of peacefulness of the victim offered by the prosecution in a homicide case to rebut evidence that the victim was the first aggressor;

(3) **Character of witness.** Evidence of the character of a witness, as provided in rules 607, 608, and 609.

(b) **Other crimes, wrongs, or acts.** Evidence of other crimes, wrongs, or acts is not admissible to prove the character of a person in order to show that he acted in conformity therewith. It may, however, be admissible for other purposes, such as proof of motive, opportunity, intent, preparation, plan, knowledge, identity, or absence of mistake or accident.

COMMENT: The second sentence of subdivision (b) as submitted to the Congress began with the words, "This subdivision does not exclude the evidence when offered." The House Committee on the Judiciary amended this language to read, in the words of the 1971 Advisory Committee draft, "it may, however, be admissable" on the ground that this formulation properly based greater emphasis on admissibility than did the final Court version.

The Advisory Committee note to this rule explains that once the admissibility of character evidence in some form is established under the rule, reference must then be made to Rule 405 in order to determine the appropriate method of proof. If the character is that of a witness, Rules 608 and 610 determine the methods of proof. In most jurisdictions today, the Advisory Committee points out, the circumstantial use of character is rejected but with important exceptions. The pattern of exceptions is incorporated in Rule 404. While its basis lies more in history and in experience than in logic, an underlying justification can fairly be found in terms of the relative presence and absence of prejudice in the various situations. In any event, the criminal rule is so deeply imbedded in our jurisprudence as to assume almost constitutional proportions and to override doubts of the basic relevancy of the evidence.

The limitation to pertinent traits of character rather than character generally in paragraphs (1) and (2) is in accordance with the prevailing view.

As to subdivision (b) the Advisory Committee emphasizes that the rule provides no mechanical solutions. The determination that must be made is whether the danger of undue prejudice outweighs the probative value of the evidence in view of the availability of other means of proof or other factors appropriate for making decisions of this kind under Rule 403 (a) .

This view of the Advisory Committee is echoed by the Senate Committee on the Judiciary. The report of the Senate Committee "anticipates that the use of the discretionary word 'may' with respect to the admissibility of evidence of crimes, wrongs, or acts is not intended to confer any arbitrary discretion on the trial judge. Rather, it is anticipated that with respect to permissible uses for such evidence, the trial judge may exclude it only on the basis of those considerations set forth in Rule 403, i.e., prejudice, confusion, or waste of time."

Rule 405. Methods of Proving Character

(a) **Reputation or opinion.** In all cases in which evidence of character or a trait of character of a person is admissible, proof may be made by testimony as to reputation or by testimony in the form of an opinion. On cross-examination, inquiry is allowable into relevant specific instances of conduct.

(b) **Specific instances of conduct.** In cases in which character or a trait of character of a person is an essential element of a charge, claim, or defense, proof may also be made of specific instances of his conduct.

COMMENT: This rule, as adopted, is the same as submitted by the Supreme Court. The Advisory Committee note explains that of the three methods of proving character provided by the rule, evidence of specific instances of conduct is the most convincing. However, it also possesses the greatest capacity to arouse prejudice, to confuse, to surprise, and to consume time. Consequently the rule confines the use of evidence of this kind to cases in which character is, in the strict sense, in issue and hence deserving of a searching inquiry. When character is used circumstantially and hence occupies a lesser status in the case, proof may be only by reputation and opinion.

The Advisory Committee also points out that in recognizing opinions as a means of proving character the rule departs from usual contemporary practice in favor of the practice of an earlier day.

In the majority of cases, on cross-examination inquiry is allowable as to whether the reputation witness has heard of the particular instances of conduct pertinent to the trait in question. The theory is that, since the reputation witness relates what he has heard, the inquiry tends to shed light on the accuracy of his hearing and reporting. Accordingly, the opinion witness would be asked whether he knew, as well as whether he had heard. The fact is, of course, that these distinctions are of slight if any practical significance, and the second sentence of subdivision (a) eliminates them as a factor in formulating questions. This recognition of the propriety of inquiring into specific instances of conduct does not otherwise circumscribe inquiry into the bases of opinion and reputation testimony.

Though Congress enacted the rule as submitted by the Court, the House had proposed to change the rule by deleting from it, as well as from Rule 608 (a), reference to opinion testimony. The House Committee report expressed the fear that wholesale allowance of opinion testimony might tend to turn a trial into a swearing contest between conflicting character witnesses.

Rule 406. Habits; Routine Practice

Evidence of the habit of a person or of the routine practice of an organization, whether corroborated or not and regardless of the presence of eyewitnesses, is relevant to prove that the conduct of the person or organization on a particular occasion was in conformity with the habit or routine practice.

COMMENT: Rule 406 as submitted to Congress contained a subdivision (b) providing that the method of proof of habit or routine practice could be "in the form of an opinion or by specific instances of conduct sufficient in number to warrant a finding that the habit existed or that the practice was routine." The House Committee on the Judiciary deleted this provision in the belief that the method of proof of habit and routine practice should be left to the courts to deal with on a case-by-case basis. At the same time, the Committee comment included the caveat that it did not intend its action to be construed as sanctioning a general authorization of opinion evidence in this area.

Thus, the rule as finally adopted is identical to Rule 406 (a) as submitted by the Court. The Advisory Committee note to this section points out that the rule is consistent with prevailing views. Disagreement, according to the Advisory Committee, generally has focused upon the question of what constitutes habit. It cites McCORMICK ON EVIDENCE § 162 at 340, for the definition of habit as "one's regular response to a repeated specific situation." Equivalent behavior on the part of a group is designated "routine practice of an organization" in the rule.

A fairly large number of authorities have required that evidence of the routine practice of an organization be corroborated as a condition precedent to its admission in evidence. This requirement, the Advisory Committee explains, is specifically rejected by the rule on the ground that it relates to the sufficiency of the evidence rather than admissibility.

Rule 407. Subsequent Remedial Measures

When, after an event, measures are taken which, if taken previously, would have made the event less likely to occur, evidence of the subsequent measures is not admissible to prove negligence or culpable conduct in connection with the event. This rule does not require the exclusion of evidence of subsequent measures when offered for another purpose, such as proving ownership, control, or feasibility of precautionary measures, if controverted, or impeachment.

COMMENT: This rule as adopted by Congress is the same as the rule submitted to it by the Supreme Court.

The Advisory Committee note indicates that the rule incorporates conventional doctrine excluding evidence of subsequent remedial measures as proof of an admission of fault. The courts, the Committee continues, have applied this principle to exclude evidence of subsequent repairs, installation of safety devices, changes in company rules, and discharge of employees, and the language of the present rule is broad enough to encompass all of them.

The second sentence, the Committee points out, directs attention to the limitations of the rule. Exclusion is called for only when the evidence of subsequent remedial measures is offered as proof of negligence or culpable conduct. In effect, the rule rejects the suggested inference that fault is admitted. Admission for other purposes is, however, allowable. Such purposes include proof of ownership or control, existence of duty, and feasibility of precautionary measures, if controverted, and impeachment.

Rule 408. Compromise and Offers to Compromise

Evidence of (1) furnishing or offering or promising to furnish, or (2) accepting or offering or promising to accept, a valuable consideration in compromising or attempting to compromise a claim which was disputed as to either validity or amount, is not admissible to prove liability for or invalidity of the claim or its amount. Evidence of conduct or statements made in compromise negotiations is likewise not admissible. This rule does not require the exclusion of any evidence otherwise discoverable merely because it is presented in the course of compromise negotiations. This rule also does not require exclusion when the evidence is offered for another purpose, such as proving bias or prejudice of a witness, negativing a contention of undue delay, or proving an effort to obstruct a criminal investigation or prosecution.

COMMENT: Congress substantially changed Rule 408 as submitted to it by the Court. The House Committee on the Judiciary first recast the rule so that admissions of liability or opinions given during compromise negotiations continue to be inadmissible, but evidence of unqualified factual assertions would be admissible. The latter aspect of the rule was drafted in the House, however, to preserve other possible objections to the introduction of such evidence. The Committee declared its intent not to modify current law whereby a party may protect himself from future use of his statements by couching them in hypothetical conditional form.

However, the Senate Committee on the Judiciary deleted the House amendment and restored the rule to the version submitted by the Supreme Court with an additional amendment. This amendment adds a sentence to insure that evidence—for example, documents—if in some other way discoverable is not rendered inadmissible merely because it is presented in the course of compromise negotiations. A party should not, the Senate Committee report declares, be able to immunize from admissibility documents otherwise discoverable merely by offering them in a compromise negotiation.

The Conference Committee report emphasizes that the House bill was drafted to meet the objection of executive agencies that under the rule as proposed by the Supreme Court a party could present a fact during compromise negotiations and thereby prevent an opposing party from offering evidence of that fact at trial even though such evidence was obtained from independent sources. The Senate amendment, which was incorporated in the final act, expressly precludes this result.

Rule 409. Payment of Medical and Similar Expenses

Evidence of furnishing or offering or promising to pay medical, hospital, or similar expenses occasioned by an injury is not admissible to prove liability for the injury.

COMMENT: This rule was enacted as submitted by the Court. The considerations underlying this rule, the Advisory Committee note asserts, parallel those underlying Rules 407 and 408. However, contrary to Rule 408, this rule does not extend to conduct or statements not a part of the act of furnishing or offering or promising to pay. This difference in treatment arises from fundamental differences in nature. Communication is essential if compromises are to be affected and consequently broad protection of statements is needed. This is not so in cases of payments or offers or promises to pay medical expenses, where factual statements may be expected to be incidental in nature.

Rule 410. Offer to Plead Guilty; Nolo Contendere; Withdrawn Plea of Guilty

Except as otherwise provided by Act of Congress, evidence of a plea of guilty, later withdrawn, or a plea of nolo contendere, or of an offer to plead guilty or nolo contendere to the crime charged or any other crime, or of statements made in connection with any of the foregoing pleas or offers, is not admissible in any civil or criminal action, case, or proceeding against the person who made the plea or offer. This rule shall not apply to the introduction of voluntary and reliable statements made in court on the record in connection with any of the foregoing pleas or offers where offered for impeachment purposes or in a subsequent prosecution of the declarant for perjury or false statement.

This rule shall not take effect until August 1, 1975, and shall be superseded by any amendment to the Federal Rules of Criminal Procedure which is inconsistent with this rule, and which takes effect after the date of the enactment of the Act establishing these Federal Rules of Evidence.

COMMENT: This rule was substantially changed before its passage by Congress. The House bill provided that evidence of a guilty or nolo contendere plea, or an offer of either plea, or statements made in connection with such pleas or offers of such pleas would be inadmissible in any civil or criminal action, case, or proceeding against the person making such plea or offer. The Senate amended this version to make the rule inapplicable to a voluntary and reliable statement made in open court on the record where the statement is offered in a subsequent prosecution of the declarant for perjury or false statement.

However, the conference committee report takes notice of the fact that the issues raised by Rule 410 also are raised by proposed Rule 11 (e) (6) of the FEDERAL RULES OF CRIMINAL PROCEDURE, which is pending before Congress. The conferees expressed their intent to make no change in the existing case law until Rule 11 (e) (6) takes effect on August 1, 1975. They further determined that the issues presented on the use of guilty and nolo contendere pleas, or offers of such pleas, and statements made in connection with such pleas or offers can be explored in greater detail during congressional consideration of Rule 11 (e) (6). Thus, the rule as finally enacted incorporates the Senate amendment plus a proviso that Rule 410 shall not take effect until August 1, 1975, and shall be superseded by any amendment to the FEDERAL RULES OF CRIMINAL PROCEDURE which is inconsistent with Rule 410, and which takes effect after the date of the enactment of the FEDERAL RULES OF EVIDENCE.

Rule 411. Liability Insurance

Evidence that a person was or was not insured against liability is not admissible upon the issue whether he acted negligently or otherwise wrongfully. This rule does not require the exclusion of evidence of insurance against liability when offered for another purpose, such as proof of agency, ownership, or control, or bias or prejudice of a witness.

COMMENT: This rule stands as submitted by the Supreme Court.

The note of the Advisory Committee emphasizes that the courts have with substantial unanimity rejected evidence of liability insurance for the purpose of proving fault and absence of liability insurance as proof of lack of fault. The note points out that the rule has been drafted in broad terms in order to include contributory negligence or other fault of a plaintiff as well as fault of a defendant. The limitations contained in the second sentence of the rule incorporate well-established illustrations.

ARTICLE V. PRIVILEGES

Rule 501. General Rule

Except as otherwise required by the Constitution of the United States or provided by Act of Congress or in rules prescribed by the Supreme Court pursuant to statutory authority, the privilege of a witness, person, government, State, or political subdivision thereof shall be governed by the principles of the common law as they may be interpreted by the courts of the United States in the light of reason and experience. However, in civil actions and proceedings, with respect to an element of a claim or defense as to which State law supplies the rule of decision, the privilege of a witness, person, government, State, or political subdivision thereof shall be determined in accordance with State law.

COMMENT: As submitted by the Supreme Court, Article V consisted of Rules 501-513, which defined specific nonconstitutional privileges to be recognized in the federal courts, such as required reports, lawyer-client, psychotherapist-patient, husband-wife, communciations to clergymen, political vote, trade secrets, secrets of state, and identity of an informer. The House Committee eliminated all of the proposed rules on specific privileges. It substituted a single rule, 501, which left the law of privileges in its present state and further provided that privileges shall continue to be developed by the courts of the United States on a uniform standard applicable both in civil and criminal cases. That standard, derived from Rule 26 of the FEDERAL RULES OF CRIMINAL PROCEDURE, mandates the application of the principles of the common law as interpreted by the courts of the United States in the light of reason and experience. The House Committee also included a proviso designed to require the application of state privilege law in civil actions and proceedings governed by *Erie Railroad Co. v. Tompkins,* 304 U.S. 64 (1938). The rationale underlying the proviso is that federal law should not supersede that of the states in substantive areas such as privilege without a compelling reason. The House Committee provision was adopted.

The Senate Committee was concerned that the language used in the House amendment could be difficult to apply and was "pregnant with litigious mischief." Therefore it proposed an amendment to provide that in criminal and federal-question cases, federally evolved rules on privilege should apply since it is a federal policy which is being enforced. Conversely, in diversity cases, where the litigation in question turns on a substantive question of state law and is brought in the federal courts because the parties reside in different states, the Senate Committee believed it clear that state rules of privilege should apply unless the proof is directed at a claim or defense for which federal law supplies the rule of decision.

The Senate Committee also observed that in approving a general rule about privileges, Congress should not be understood as disapproving any recognition of a psychiatrist-patient, husband-wife, or any other privilege enumerated in the Supreme Court rules. Rather, congressional action should be understood as reflecting the view that the recognition of a privilege based on a confidential relationship and the recognition of other types of privileges should be determined on a case-by-case basis.

In effect, Rule 501 as enacted leaves privileges created by state law effective in diversity cases but not in other federal cases such as criminal, federal-question, and bankruptcy cases.

As explained by the Conference Committee Report,

"state privilege law would usually apply in diversity cases. There may be diversity cases, however, where a claim or defense is based upon federal law. In such instances, federal privilege law will apply to evidence relevant to the federal claim or defense. . . . In nondiversity jurisdiction civil cases, federal privilege law will generally apply. In those situations where a federal court adopts or incorporates state law to fill interstices or gaps in federal statutory phrases, the court generally will apply federal privilege law."

ARTICLE VI.   WITNESSES

Rule 601. General Rule of Competency

Every person is competent to be a witness except as otherwise
provided in these rules. However, in civil actions and proceedings,
with respect to an element of a claim or defense as to which State law
supplies the rule of decision, the competency of a witness shall be
determined in accordance with State law.

COMMENT: As submitted by the Supreme Court this rule stated only
that every person is competent to be a witness, except as otherwise provided in the rules. This general ground-clearing, the Advisory Committee
note explains, eliminates all grounds of incompetence not specifically recognized in the succeeding rules of Article VI. In particular, the rule as
submitted by the Court would have rendered state Dead Man's Acts inapplicable in federal litigation. However, the House amended Rule 601
to provide that in civil actions and proceedings state competency law
applies "to an element of a claim or defense as to which state law supplies
the rule of decision." The Senate Committee in turn provided that

"in civil actions and proceedings arising under 28 U.S.C. Sec. 1332
or 28 U.S.C. 1335, or between citizens of different states and renewed
under 28 U.S.C. Sec. 1441 (b) the competency of a witness, person,
government, state or political subdivision thereof is determined in
accordance with state law, unless with respect to the particular claim
or defense, federal law supplies the rule of decision."

These approaches mirrored the House and Senate Committee proposals
with respect to Rule 501. The Conference Committee, for reasons similar
to those underlying its actions on Rule 501, adopted the House provision.

Rule 602. Lack of Personal Knowledge

A witness may not testify to a matter unless evidence is introduced sufficient to support a finding that he has personal knowledge
of the matter. Evidence to prove personal knowledge may, but need
not, consist of the testimony of the witness himself. This rule is subject to the provisions of rule 703, relating to opinion testimony by
expert witnesses.

COMMENT: Rule 602 was adopted as submitted by the Court. The
Advisory Committee note points out that Rule 602 is in fact a specialized

application of the provisions of Rule 104 (b) on conditional relevancy. Rule 602 does not govern the situation of a witness who testifies to a hearsay statement as such, if he has personal knowledge of the making of the statement. Rules 801 and 805 would be applicable in that situation. Rule 602 would, however, prevent a witness from testifying to the subject matter of the hearsay statement, since he has no personal knowledge of it.

The reference to Rule 703 is designed to avoid any question of conflict between Rule 602 and Rule 703, the latter of which allows an expert to express opinions based on facts not known personally to him.

Rule 603. Oath or Affirmation

Before testifying, every witness shall be required to declare that he will testify truthfully, by oath or affirmation administered in a form calculated to awaken his conscience and impress his mind with his duty to do so.

COMMENT: Rule 603 was adopted in the form submitted by the Court. The Advisory Committee note indicates that this rule was designed to afford the flexibility required in dealing with religious adults, atheists, conscientious objectors, mental defectives, and children. Affirmation is simply a solemn undertaking to tell the truth and requires no special verbal formula.

Rule 604. Interpreters

An interpreter is subject to the provisions of these rules relating to qualification as an expert and the administration of an oath or affirmation that he will make a true translation.

COMMENT: Rule 604 was adopted as submitted by the Court. The Advisory Committee note to this rule simply observes that Rule 604 is an implementation of FED. R. CIV. P. 43 (f) and FED. R. CRIM. P. 28 (b), both of which sections contain provisions for the appointment and compensation of interpreters.

Rule 605. Competency of Judge as Witness

The judge presiding at the trial may not testify in that trial as a witness. No objection need be made in order to preserve the point.

COMMENT: Rule 605 was adopted in the form submitted by the Court. The Advisory Committee note to Rule 605 acknowledges that the likelihood of a federal judge being called to testify in a trial over which he is presiding is slight. The solution incorporated to eliminate even this slight possibility is a broad rule of incompetency.

The rule also provides for an "automatic" objection. To require an actual objection would confront the opponent with the choice between not objecting, with the result of allowing the testimony, and objecting, with the probable result of excluding the testimony, but at the price of continuing the trial before a judge likely to feel that his integrity had been attacked by the objector.

Rule 606. Competency of Juror as Witness

(a) At the trial. A member of the jury may not testify as a witness before that jury in the trial of the case in which he is sitting as a juror. If he is called so to testify, the opposing party shall be afforded an opportunity to object out of the presence of the jury.

(b) Inquiry into validity of verdict or indictment. Upon an inquiry into the validity of a verdict or indictment, a juror may not testify as to any matter or statement occurring during the course of the jury's deliberations or to the effect of anything upon his or any other juror's mind or emotions as influencing him to assent to or dissent from the verdict or indictment or concerning his mental processes in connection therewith, except that a juror may testify on the question whether extraneous prejudicial information was improperly brought to the jury's attention or whether any outside influence was improperly brought to bear upon any juror. Nor may his affidavit or evidence of any statement by him concerning a matter about what he would be precluded from testifying be received for these purposes.

COMMENT: Rule 606 (a) was adopted without change by the Congress. The Advisory Committee note to subdivision (a) observes that testimony by a juror in a trial in which he is sitting as a juror bears an obvious similarity to testimony by a sitting judge. However, the judge, the Committee continues, is not in this instance so involved as to call for departure from usual principles requiring objection to be made; hence, the only provision on objection is that opportunity be afforded for its making out of the presence of the jury.

Congressional concern centered on subdivision (b) . As received from the Court, Rule 606(b) severely limited testimony by a juror in the course of an inquiry into the validity of a verdict or indictment. The juror could testify as to the influence of extraneous prejudicial information brought to the jury's attention or an outside influence that improperly had been brought to bear upon a juror, but he could not testify as to other irregularities that occurred in the jury room. Under this fomulation, the House Committee noted, a quotient verdict could not be attacked on the testimony of a juror, nor could a juror testify to the drunken condition of a fellow juror which so disabled that juror as to prevent him from participating in jury deliberations. The House Committee in effect amended subdivision (b) to incorporate in the 1969 and 1971 Advisory Committee drafts language that would have permitted a member of the jury to testify concerning these kinds of irregularities in the jury room.

The Senate, however, reinstated a broader rule of incompetency so that a juror could not testify about any matter or statement occurring during the course of the jury's deliberations. As rewritten by the Senate Committee, the rule does provide, however, that a juror may testify as to whether extraneous prejudicial information was improperly brought to the jury's attention and as to whether any outside influence was improperly brought to bear on any juror.

The Conference Committee adopted the Senate amendment, believing that jurors should be encouraged to be conscientious and to promptly report to the court misconduct that occurs during jury deliberations.

The Senate Committee had explained that the House deletion of the proscription against testimony "as to any matter or statement occurring during the course of the jury's deliberations" would have the effect of opening up verdicts to challenge on the basis of what happened during the jury's internal deliberations—for example, where a juror alleged that the jury refused to follow the trial judge's instructions or that some of the jurors did not take part in deliberations. Such a rule, the Senate Committee observed, could permit the harassment of former jurors by losing parties, as well as the possible exploitation of disgruntled or otherwise badly motivated ex-jurors. Public policy, the Senate Committee continued, requires a finality to litigation. Common fairness requires that absolute privacy be preserved so that jurors may engage in the full and free debate necessary to attain just verdicts. In the interest of protecting the jury system and the citizens who make it work, the Senate Committee concluded, Rule 606 should not permit any inquiry into the internal deliberations of the jurors.

Rule 607. Who May Impeach

The credibility of a witness may be attacked by any party, including the party calling him.

COMMENT: Rule 607 was enacted by Congress as it was submitted by the Court. The Advisory Committee note to this rule emphasizes that the traditional rule against impeaching one's own witness is based on false premises and therefore has been abandoned. If the impeachment is by a prior statement, it is free from hearsay dangers and is excluded from the category of hearsay under Rule 801(d)(1).

Rule 608. Evidence of Character and Conduct of Witness

(a) **Opinion and reputation evidence of character.** The credibility of a witness may be attacked or supported by evidence in the form of opinion or reputation, but subject to these limitations: (1) the evidence may refer only to character for truthfulness or untruthfulness, and (2) evidence of truthful character is admissible only after the character of the witness for truthfulness has been attacked by opinion or reputation evidence or otherwise.

(b) **Specific instances of conduct.** Specific instances of the conduct of a witness, for the purpose of attacking or supporting his credibility, other than conviction of crime as provided in rule 609, may not be proved by extrinsic evidence. They may, however, in the discretion of the court, if probative of truthfulness or untruthfulness, be inquired into on cross-examination of the witness (1) concerning his character for truthfulness or untruthfulness, or (2) concerning the character for truthfulness or untruthfulness of another witness as to which character the witness being cross-examined has testified.

The giving of testimony, whether by an accused or by any other witness, does not operate as a waiver of his privilege against self-incrimination when examined with respect to matters which relate only to credibility.

COMMENT: With the exception of the second sentence of subdivision (b), Rule 608 was adopted as submitted by the Court.

The Advisory Committee note to subdivision (a) points out that this rule develops the exception to Rule 404(a) that character evidence bearing upon the credibility of a witness is admissible. "In accordance with the bulk of judicial authority the inquiry is strictly limited to character for veracity, rather than allowing evidence as to character generally." The result, according to the Advisory Committee, is to sharpen relevency; to reduce surprise, waste of time, and confusion; and to make the lot of the witness somewhat less unattractive.

The permitted use of opinion and reputation evidence as a means of proving the character of witnesses is consistent with Rule 405(a).

Except when the witness is the accused testifying on his own behalf, character evidence in support of witness credibility is admissible under the rule only after the character of the witness has first been attacked, as has been the case at common law. Opinion or reputation that the witness is untruthful specifically qualifies as an attack under the rule, and evidence of misconduct, including conviction of crime, and of corruption also falls within this category, but evidence of bias or interest does not. Whether evidence in the form of contradiction is an attack upon the character of the witness must depend upon the circumstances. The exception with respect to the accused who testifies is based upon the assumption that the mere circumstance of being the accused is an attack on character. It is consistent with the admissibility of evidence of good character under Rule 404(a)(1).

The second sentence of Rule 608 (b) as submitted by the Court permitted specific instances of misconduct on the part of a witness to be inquired into on cross-examination for the purpose of attacking witness credibility, if probative of truthfulness or untruthfulness and "not remote in time." Such cross-examination could be of the witness himself or of another witness who testifies as to "his" character for truthfulness or untruthfulness. The House Committee amended the rule to emphasize the discretionary power of the court in permitting such testimony and deleted the reference to remoteness in time as being unnecessary and confusing (remoteness from time of trial or remoteness from the incident involved?). As recast, the Committee amendment also makes clear the antecedent of "his" in the original Court proposal.

Rule 609. Impeachment by Evidence of Conviction of Crime

(a) **General rule.** For the purpose of attacking the credibility of a witness, evidence that he has been convicted of a crime shall be admitted if elicited from him or established by public record during cross-examination but only if the crime (1) was punishable by death or imprisonment in excess of one year under the law under which he was convicted, and the court determines that the probative value of admitting this evidence outweighs its prejudicial effect to the defendant, or (2) involved dishonesty or false statement, regardless of the punishment.

(b) **Time limit.** Evidence of a conviction under this rule is not admissible if a period of more than ten years has elapsed since the date of the conviction or of the release of the witness from the confinement imposed for that conviction, whichever is the later date, unless the court determines, in the interests of justice, that the probative value of the conviction supported by specific facts and circumstances substantially outweighs its prejudicial effect. However, evidence of a conviction more than 10 years old as calculated herein, is not admissible unless the proponent gives to the adverse party sufficient advance written notice of intent to use such evidence to provide the adverse party with a fair opportunity to contest the use of such evidence.

(c) **Effect of pardon, annulment, or certificate of rehabilitation.** Evidence of a conviction is not admissible under this rule if (1) the conviction has been the subject of a pardon, annulment, certificate of rehabilitation, or other equivalent procedure based on a finding of the rehabilitation of the person convicted, and that person has not been convicted of a subsequent crime which was punishable by death or imprisonment in excess of one year, or (2) the conviction has been the subject of a pardon, annulment, or other equivalent procedure based on a finding of innocence.

(d) **Juvenile adjudications.** Evidence of juvenile adjudications is generally not admissible under this rule. The court may, however, in a criminal case allow evidence of a juvenile adjudication of a witness other than the accused if conviction of the offense would be admissible to attack the credibility of an adult and the court is satisfied that admission in evidence is necessary for a fair determination of the issue of guilt or innocence.

(e) **Pendency of appeal.** The pendency of an appeal therefrom does not render evidence of a conviction inadmissible. Evidence of the pendency of an appeal is admissible.

COMMENT: Rule 609 (a) as submitted by the Court provided that the credibility of a witness could be attacked by evidence that he had been convicted of a crime if the crime was punishable by death or by imprisonment in excess of one year under the law under which he was convicted or involved dishonesty or false statement regardless of punishment. The House Committee amended this provision to permit an attack upon the credibility of a witness by evidence of prior conviction only if the prior crime involved dishonesty or false statement.

The Senate Committee adopted a modified version of the House-passed rule. With respect to defendants, the Senate Committee agreed with the House limitation that only "offenses involving false statement or dishonesty" may be used. By that phrase the Senate Committee intended to cover crimes such as perjury or subornation of perjury, false statements, criminal fraud, embezzlement or false pretense, or any other offense, in the nature of *crimen falsi,* the commission of which involves some element of untruthfulness, deceit, or falsification bearing on the accused's propensity to testify truthfully. With respect to other witnesses, in addition to any prior conviction involving false statement or dishonesty, any other felony could be used to impeach if and only if the court found that the probative value of such evidence outweighed its prejudicial effect against the party offering that witness.

The Conference Committee adopted the Senate amendment with an amendment. The Conference amendment provides that the credibility of a witness, whether a defendant or someone else, may be attacked by proof of the prior conviction but only if the crime: (1) was punishable by death or by imprisonment in excess of one year under the law under which he was convicted and the court determines that the probative value of the conviction outweighs its prejudicial effect to the defendant; (2) involved dishonesty or false statement regardless of the punishment. The admission of prior convictions involving dishonesty and false statement is not within the discretion of the court. The Conference Committee report points out that such convictions are peculiarly probative of credibility and, under this rule, are always to be admitted. Thus, judicial discretion granted with respect to the admissibility of other prior convictions is not applicable to those involving dishonesty or false statement.

Rule 609(b) as submitted by the Court would have rendered evidence of a conviction inadmissible if a period of more than 10 years had elapsed since the date of the release of the witness from confinement imposed for his most recent conviction, or the expiration of the period of his parole, probation, or sentence granted or imposed with respect to his most recent conviction, whichever is the later date. The House Committee objected that under this formulation, a witness' entire past record of criminal convictions could be used for impeachment if the witness had been most recently released from confinement, or the period of his parole or probation had expired, within 10 years of conviction. Therefore, the Committee amended the rule to incorporate the text of the 1971 Advisory Committee version, which provided that upon the expiration of 10 years from the date of the conviction of the witness for an offense, or of his release from confinement for that offense, that conviction may no longer be used for impeachment.

However, the Senate Committee amended subdivision (b) to permit the use of convictions older than 10 years, if the court determined, in the interest of justice, that the probative value of the conviction, supported by specific facts and circumstances, substantially outweighed its prejudicial effect.

The Conference Committee adopted the Senate amendment with an amendment requiring notice by a party that he intends to request that the court allow him to use a conviction older than 10 years. The Conference Committee report noted that the rule as amended anticipated that the written notice, in order to give the adversary a full opportunity to contest the use of the evidence, would ordinarily include such information as the date of the conviction, the jurisdiction, and the offense or statute involved. The Senate Committee report with respect to the Senate amendment emphasized that convictions over 10 years old are intended to be admitted very rarely and only in exceptional circumstances. The court is required by the rule to make specific findings on the record as to the particular facts and circumstances it has considered in determining that the probative value of the conviction substantially outweighs its prejudicial impact. The Senate Committee also expects that, in fairness, the court will give the party against whom the conviction is introduced a full and adequate opportunity to contest its admission.

Rule 609 (c) as submitted by the Court provided that evidence of a witness' prior conviction is not admissible to attack his credibility if the conviction was the subject of a pardon, annulment, or other equivalent procedure based on a showing of rehabilitation, and the witness has not been convicted of a subsequent crime. The House Committee amended the rule to provide that the "subsequent crime" must have been "punishable by death or imprisonment in excess of one year," on the ground that a subsequent conviction of an offense not a felony is insufficient to rebut the finding that the witness has been rehabilitated. The Committee also noted its intention that the words "based on a finding of the rehabilitation of the person convicted" apply not only to "certificate of rehabilitation, or other equivalent procedure," but also to "pardon" and "annulment."

Subdivision (d) was adopted substantially as submitted by the Court. The Advisory Committee note to this subdivision indicates that the prevailing view has been that a juvenile adjudication is not usable for impeachment. Subdivision (d) recognizes the discretion of the judge, in extraordinary circumstances, to depart from this general principle of exclusion. In deference to the general pattern and policy of juvenile statutes, however, no discretion is accorded when the witness is the accused in a criminal case.

Subdivision (e) was adopted as submitted by the Court.

Rule 610. Religious Beliefs or Opinions

Evidence of the beliefs or opinions of a witness on matters of religion is not admissible for the purpose of showing that by reason of their nature his credibility is impaired or enhanced.

COMMENT: This rule was adopted as submitted by the Court. The Advisory Committee note explains that while the rule forecloses inquiry into the religious beliefs or opinions of a witness for the purpose of showing that his character for truthfulness is affected by their nature, an inquiry for the purpose of showing interest or bias because of them is not within the prohibition. Thus, disclosure of affiliation with a church which is a party to the litigation would be allowable under the rule.

Rule 611. Mode and Order of Interrogation and Presentation

(a) **Control by court.** The court shall exercise reasonable control over the mode and order of interrogating witnesses and presenting evidence so as to (1) make the interrogation and presentation effective for the ascertainment of the truth, (2) avoid needless consumption of time, and (3) protect witnesses from harassment or undue embarrassment.

(b) **Scope of cross-examination.** Cross-examination should be limited to the subject matter of the direct examination and matters affecting the credibility of the witness. The court may, in the exercise of discretion, permit inquiry into additional matters as if on direct examination.

(c) **Leading questions.** Leading questions should not be used on the direct examination of a witness except as may be necessary to develop his testimony. Ordinarily leading questions should be permitted on cross-examination. When a party calls a hostile witness, an adverse party, or a witness identified with an adverse party, interrogation may be by leading questions.

COMMENT: Subdivision (a) of this rule was adopted by Congress substantially as submitted by the Court.

Item (1) of this subdivision, the Advisory Committee note asserts, restates in broad terms judicial power and obligation developed under common law principles. Item (2), addressed to avoiding needless use of time, complements Rule 403, which vests in the judge discretion to exclude evidence as a waste of time. Considerations pertinent to item (3) include the importance of the testimony, the nature of the inquiry, and the inquiry's relevance to credibility, waste of time, and confusion. The inquiry into specific instances of witness conduct allowed under Rule 608 (b) is, of course, subject to this rule.

Subdivision (b) as submitted by the Supreme Court permitted great latitude in cross-examination, which might extend to "any matter relevant to any issue in the case," unless the judge, in the interests of justice, limited its scope. The House narrowed the rule to the more traditional practice of limiting cross-examination to the subject matter of direct examination (and credibility), but allowed the judge discretion to permit inquiry into additional matters and situations where inquiry would aid in development of the evidence or otherwise facilitate the conduct of the trial. The House Committee report noted that this traditional rule facilitated orderly presentation by each party at trial and further stated that in light of existing discovery procedures, there appeared to be no need to abandon the traditional rule.

The Senate Committee concurred in this restriction of the scope of cross-examination with the understanding that the limitation would not preclude the utilization of leading questions if the conditions of subdivision (c) of Rule 611 were met, bearing in mind the judge's discretion in any case to limit the scope of cross-examination. The Senate Committee report also expressed the opinion that the rule as reported by the House was flexible enough to provide sufficiently broad cross-examination in appropriate situations in multi-district litigation. This view is in direct contradiction to that expressed by the federal judges who make up the Board of Editors of the Manual for Complex Litiga-tion. These judges are of the belief that the rule as adopted by the House would have a "harmful and crippling effect on efficient processing of multi-district and other complex litigation."

The third sentence of Rule 611(c) as submitted by the Court provided that: "In civil cases, a party is entitled to call an adverse witness or witness identified with him and interrogate by leading questions." The House Committee amended this subdivision to permit leading questions to be asked of any hostile witness. It also substituted the term "when" for "in civil cases" to reflect the possibility that in criminal cases a defendant may be entitled to call witnesses identified with the Government, in which event the defendant should be permitted to ask leading questions.

The Senate Committee report questioned whether the addition of the term "hostile witness" by the House was necessary. The Advisory Committee note explaining the subdivision clearly intended, it pointed out, that leading questions could be asked of a hostile witness or a witness who was unwilling or biased even if that witness was not associated with an adverse party. The Senate Committee nevertheless concurred in the House version, concluding that the change was intended solely to clarify the fact that leading questions are permissible in the interrogation of a witness who is hostile in fact. The Senate Committee also accepted the House extension of the subdivision to criminal as well as civil cases, but urged that this extension of the rule be applied with caution.

Rule 612. Writing Used to Refresh Memory

Except as otherwise provided in criminal proceedings by section 3500 of title 18, United States Code, if a witness uses a writing to refresh his memory for the purpose of testifying, either—

(1) while testifying, or

CANISIUS COLLEGE LIBRARY
BUFFALO, N. Y.

(2) before testifying, if the court in its discretion determines
it is necessary in the interests of justice,
an adverse party is entitled to have the writing produced at the hearing, to inspect it, to cross-examine the witness thereon, and to introduce in evidence those portions which relate to the testimony of the
witness. If it is claimed that the writing contains matters not related
to the subject matter of the testimony the court shall examine the
writing in camera, excise any portions not so related, and order
delivery of the remainder to the party entitled thereto. Any portion
withheld over objections shall be preserved and made available to
the appellate court in the event of an appeal. If a writing is not produced or delivered pursuant to order under this rule, the court shall
make any order justice requires, except that in criminal cases when
the prosecution elects not to comply, the order shall be one striking
the testimony or, if the court in its discretion determines that the
interests of justice so require, declaring a mistrial.

COMMENT: This rule as submitted by the Court made no distinction
between writings used to refresh recollection while the witness was on
the stand and those used before the witness took the stand. The House
Committee amended the rule so that it still required the production of
writings used by a witness while testifying, but left to the court's discretion whether the witness had to produce the writings used to refresh his
memory before testifying. The House Committee report asserted that
permitting an adverse party to require the production of writings used
before testifying could result in fishing expeditions among a multitude
of papers that a witness might have used in preparing for trial. The
House Committee added that nothing in the rule should be construed as
barring the assertion of a privilege with respect to writings used by a
witness to refresh his memory.

Rule 613. Prior Statements of Witnesses

(a) **Examining witness concerning prior statement.** In examining a witness concerning a prior statement made by him, whether
written or not, the statement need not be shown nor its contents disclosed to him at that time, but on request the same shall be shown or
disclosed to opposing counsel.

(b) **Extrinsic evidence of prior inconsistent statement of witness.**
Extrinsic evidence of a prior inconsistent statement by a witness is
not admissible unless the witness is afforded an opportunity to explain or deny the same and the opposite party is afforded an oppor-

tunity to interrogate him thereon, or the interests of justice otherwise require. This provision does not apply to admissions of a party-opponent as defined in rule 801 (d) (2).

COMMENT: This rule was adopted as submitted by the Supreme Court.

The Advisory Committee note to subdivision (a) points out that this provision for disclosure to counsel is designed to forestall unwarranted insinuations that a statement has been made when the fact is to the contrary. The rule does not, the Advisory Committee declares, defeat the application of Rule 1002, which requires the production of the original to prove the contents of a writing. Nor does it defeat the application of FED. R. CIV. P. 26 (b) (3), which entitles a person on request to a copy of his own statement, though it may temporarily suspend the operation of this civil practice rule.

With respect to subdivision (b), the Advisory Committee observes that the traditional insistence upon directing the attention of the witness to the prior statement on cross-examination is relaxed in favor of simply providing the witness an opportunity to explain and providing the opposite party an opportunity to examine the witness on the statement, with no specification of any particular time or sequence. Under this procedure, several collusive witnesses can be examined before disclosure of a prior joint statement that was inconsistent. In order to allow for the possibility that the witness might be unavailable by the time the statement is discovered, and for other possibilities of a like nature, a measure of discretion is conferred upon the judge.

Under principles of *expressio unius* the rule does not apply to impeachment by evidence of prior inconsistent conduct. The use of inconsistent statements to impeach a hearsay declaration is treated in Rule 806.

Rule 614. Calling and Interrogation of Witnesses by Court

(a) **Calling by court.** The court may, on its own motion or at the suggestion of a party, call witnesses, and all parties are entitled to cross-examine witnesses thus called.

(b) **Interrogation by court.** The court may interrogate witnesses, whether called by itself or by a party.

(c) **Objections.** Objections to the calling of witnesses by the court or to interrogation by it may be made at the time or at the next available opportunity when the jury is not present.

COMMENT: Rule 614 was adopted as submitted by the Court.
The note of the Advisory Committee to subdivision (a) of this

rule emphasizes that the authority of a judge to call witnesses is well established in both criminal and civil cases.

The authority of the judge to question a witness, as set out in subdivision (b), is also well established. But, the Committee states, the authority is abused if the judge abandons his proper role and assumes that of an advocate. Nevertheless, the Advisory Committee believes that the manner in which interrogation should be conducted and the proper extent of its exercise cannot be formulated in a rule. The failure to provide a formula for conducting interrogation in subdivision (b) in no sense precludes courts of review from continuing to reverse for abuse.

Subdivision (c) on objections is designed to relieve counsel of the embarrassment attendant upon objecting to questions by the judge in the presence of the jury. At the same time, it assures that objections are made in sufficient time to afford the opportunity to take possible corrective measures.

Rule 615. Exclusion of Witnesses

At the request of a party the court shall order witnesses excluded so that they cannot hear the testimony of other witnesses, and it may make the order of its own motion. This rule does not authorize exclusion of (1) a party who is a natural person, or (2) an officer or employee of a party which is not a natural person designated as its representative by its attorney, or (3) a person whose presence is shown by a party to be essential to the presentation of his cause.

COMMENT: This rule was adopted as submitted by the Court. The Advisory Committee note to the rule stresses that the authority of the judge to sequester witnesses is admitted, but there is a question as to whether sequestration is a matter of discretion or of right. The rule takes the latter position, making it mandatory for the judge to sequester witnesses if requested to do so by a party. No time is specified for making the request. The Advisory Committee also points out that exception (2) has been invoked to allow a police officer who has been in charge of an investigation to remain in court despite the fact that he will be a witness.

Though Congress made no changes in this rule, the Senate Committee expressed its understanding, which it deemed to be the view of the House Committee also, that the rule would be construed to bring investigative agents within the scope of exception (2).

ARTICLE VII. OPINIONS AND EXPERT TESTIMONY

Rule 701. Opinion Testimony by Lay Witnesses

If a witness is not testifying as an expert, his testimony in the form of opinions or inferences is limited to those opinions or inferences which are (a) rationally based on the perception of the witness and (b) helpful to a clear understanding of his testimony or the determination of a fact in issue.

COMMENT: This rule was adopted as submitted by the Court. The rule retains the traditional objective of putting the trier of fact in possession of an accurate reproduction of the event. According to the Advisory Committee, limitation (a) is but the familiar requirement of firsthand knowledge or observation. Limitation (b) is phrased in terms of requiring testimony to be helpful in resolving issues. The rule assumes that the natural characteristics of the adversary system will generally lead to an acceptable result, since the detailed account carries more conviction than the broad assertion, and a lawyer can be expected to display his witness to the best advantage. If, the Advisory Committee continues, despite these considerations, attempts are made to introduce meaningless assertions that amount to little more than choosing of sides, exclusion for lack of helpfulness is called for by the rule.

Rule 702. Testimony by Experts

If scientific, technical, or other specialized knowledge will assist the trier of fact to understand the evidence or to determine a fact in issue, a witness qualified as an expert by knowledge, skill, experience, training, or education, may testify thereto in the form of an opinion or otherwise.

COMMENT: This rule was adopted as submitted by the Court. The Advisory Committee note underscores the broad phrasing of the rule. The fields of knowledge that may be drawn upon are not limited merely to the "scientific" and "technical" but extend to all "specialized" knowledge. Similarly, an "expert" is viewed, not in a narrow sense, but as a person qualified by "knowledge, skill, experience, training, or education." Thus, under the rule, the "expert" group includes so-called "skilled" witnesses, such as bankers or landowners testifying to land values.

Rule 703. Bases of Opinion Testimony by Experts

The facts or data in the particular case upon which an expert bases an opinion or inference may be those perceived by or made known to him at or before the hearing. If of a type reasonably relied upon by experts in the particular field in forming opinions or inferences upon the subject, the facts or data need not be admissible in evidence.

COMMENT: This rule was adopted as submitted by the Court.

The Advisory Committee note to this rule points out that facts or data upon which expert opinions are based may be derived from three possible sources. The first source, the firsthand observation of the witness, traditionally has been allowed. The second source, presentation at the trial, also reflects existing practice. The technique of presentation may be posing the familiar hypothetical question to the expert or having him attend the trial to hear the testimony establishing the facts. The third source consists of presentation of data to the expert outside of court and by means other than his own perception. In this respect the rule is designed to broaden the basis for expert opinion beyond that current in many jurisdictions and to bring the judicial practice into line with the practice of experts themselves when not in court.

The rule also offers a more satisfactory basis, according to the Advisory Committee, for ruling upon the admissibility of public opinion poll evidence. Attention is directed to the validity of the techniques employed rather than to the relatively fruitless inquiries into whether hearsay is involved.

The Advisory Committee note also stresses that despite the expansion wrought by this rule, the facts or data must "be of a type reasonably relied upon by experts in the particular field." For example, in an auto accident case, this language, the Committee continues, would not warrant admitting in evidence on the question of the point of impact the opinion of an "accidentologist" based on statements of bystanders.

Rule 704. Opinion on Ultimate Issue

Testimony in the form of an opinion or inference otherwise admissible is not objectionable because it embraces an ultimate issue to be decided by the trier of fact.

COMMENT: This rule was adopted as submitted by the Court. The Advisory Committee note to this section indicates that, since the basic approach of the rules is to admit lay and expert opinions when helpful to the trier of fact, Rule 704 specifically abolishes the so-called ultimate-issue rule. The Committee cautions, however, that the abolition of the ultimate-issue rule does not lower the bars so as to admit all opinions. Rules 701 and 702, the Committee observes, afford ample assurances against the admission of opinions that would merely tell the jury what result to reach. They also may be used to exclude opinions phrased in terms of inadequately explored legal criteria, such as "Did T have the capacity to make a will?" On the other hand, they would allow the question, "Did T have sufficient mental capacity to know the nature and extent of his property and the natural objects of his bounty and to formulate a rational scheme of distribution?"

Rule 705. Disclosure of Facts or Data Underlying Expert Opinion

The expert may testify in terms of opinion or inference and give his reasons therefor without prior disclosure of the underlying facts or data, unless the court requires otherwise. The expert may in any event be required to disclose the underlying facts or data on cross-examination.

COMMENT: This rule was adopted as submitted by the Court.

The elimination of the requirement of preliminary disclosure of underlying facts or data at trial has a long background of support, the Advisory Committee note to this rule asserts. If it is objected that leaving it to the cross-examiner to bring out the supporting data is essentially unfair, it may be answered that the cross-examiner is under no compulsion to bring out any facts or data except those unfavorable to the opinion. Moreover, the judge has the discretionary power to require preliminary disclosure in any event.

Rule 706. Court Appointed Experts

(a) **Appointment.** The court may on its own motion or on the motion of any party enter an order to show cause why expert witnesses should not be appointed, and may request the parties to submit nominations. The court may appoint any expert witnesses agreed upon by the parties, and may appoint expert witnesses of its own selection. An expert witness shall not be appointed by the court unless he consents to act. A witness so appointed shall be informed of his duties by the court in writing, a copy of which shall be filed with the clerk, or at a conference in which the parties shall have opportunity to participate. A witness so appointed shall advise the parties of his findings, if any; his deposition may be taken by any party; and he may be called to testify by the court or any party. He shall be subject to cross-examination by each party, including a party calling him as a witness.

(b) Compensation. Expert witnesses so appointed are entitled to reasonable compensation in whatever sum the court may allow. The compensation thus fixed is payable from funds which may be provided by law in criminal cases and civil actions and proceedings involving just compensation under the Fifth Amendment. In other civil actions and proceedings the compensation shall be paid by the parties in such proportion and at such time as the court directs, and thereafter charged in like manner as other costs.

(c) Disclosure of appointment. In the exercise of its discretion, the court may authorize disclosure to the jury of the fact that the court appointed the expert witness.

(d) Parties' experts of own selection. Nothing in this rule limits the parties in calling expert witnesses of their own selection.

COMMENT: This rule was adopted as submitted by the Court.

Subdivision (a), the Advisory Committee note indicates, is based on FED. R. CRIM. P. 28, to which language has been added to provide specifically for appointment either on motion of a party or on the judge's own motion. A provision subjecting the court-appointed expert to deposition procedures has also been incorporated. Finally, the language of the original criminal procedure rule has been revised to make definite the right of any party, including the party calling the witness, to cross-examine.

Subdivision (b), according to the Advisory Committee, combines the present provision for compensation in criminal cases with a fair and feasible handling of civil cases, which combination originally was found in the Model Expert Testimony Act and carried from there into Uniform Rule 60. The special provision for fifth-amendment compensation cases is designed to guard against reducing constitutionally guaranteed just compensation by requiring the recipient to pay costs.

Subdivision (c) is deemed essential by the Advisory Committee if the use of court-appointed experts is to be fully effective.

Finally, subdivision (d) is in essence the last sentence of FED. R. CRIM. P. 28 (a).

ARTICLE VIII. HEARSAY

Rule 801. Definitions

The following definitions apply under this article:

(a) Statement. A "statement" is (1) an oral or written assertion or (2) nonverbal conduct of a person, if it is intended by him as an assertion.

(b) Declarant. A "declarant" is a person who makes a statement.

(c) Hearsay. "Hearsay" is a statement, other than one made by the declarant while testifying at the trial or hearing, offered in evidence to prove the truth of the matter asserted.

(d) Statements which are not hearsay. A statement is not hearsay if—

(1) **Prior statement by witness.** The declarant testifies at the trial or hearing and is subject to cross-examination concerning the statement, and the statement is (A) inconsistent with his testimony, and was given under oath subject to the penalty of perjury at a trial, hearing, or other proceeding, or in a deposition, or (B) consistent with his testimony and is offered to rebut an express or implied charge against him of recent fabrication or improper influence or motive, or

(2) **Admission by party-opponent.** The statement is offered against a party and is (A) his own statement, in either his individual or a representative capacity or (B) a statement of which he has manifested his adoption or belief in its truth, or (C) a statement by a person authorized by him to make a statement concerning the subject, or (D) a statement by his agent or servant concerning a matter within the scope of his agency or employment, made during the existence of the relationship, or (E) a statement by a coconspirator of a party during the course and in furtherance of the conspiracy.

COMMENT: This rule was adopted as submitted by the Court, with the exception of two amendments to subdivision (d) (1).

With respect to subdivision (a) the Advisory Committee explained that the effect of the definition of statement is to exclude from the hearsay rule all evidence of conduct, verbal or nonverbal, not intended as an assertion. The key to the definition is that nothing is an assertion unless it is intended to be one. Some nonverbal conduct, such as the act of pointing to identify a suspect in a lineup, is clearly the equivalent of words and is to be regarded as a statement. Other nonverbal conduct, however, may be offered as evidence that the person acted as he did because of his belief in the existence of the condition sought to be proved, from which belief the existence of the condition may be inferred. This sequence, it may be argued, is in effect an assertion of the existence of the condition and hence probably includable within the hearsay concept. While no class of evidence is free of the possibility of fabrication, the likelihood is less with nonverbal than with assertive verbal conduct.

When evidence of conduct is offered on the theory that it is not a statement, and hence not hearsay, a preliminary finding will be required to determine whether an assertion is intended. The rule is so worded as to place the burden upon the party claiming that the intention existed; ambiguous and doubtful cases will be resolved against him and in favor of admissibility.

Subdivision (c), the Advisory Committee says, follows familiar lines in including only statements offered to prove the truth of the matter asserted. If the significance of an offered statement lies only in the fact that it was made, no issue has been raised as to the truth of anything asserted, and the statement is not hearsay.

As submitted by the Supreme Court, subdivision (d) (1) (A) made admissible as substantive evidence the prior statement of a witness inconsistent with his present testimony. The House severely limited the admissibility of prior inconsistent statements by requiring that the prior statement must have been subjected to cross-examination, thus precluding even the use of grand jury statements. The Senate rejected the House amendment and returned the rule to the form as submitted by the Supreme Court. The Conference Committee adopted the Senate amendment with an amendment so that the rule now requires that the prior inconsistent statement be given under oath subject to penalty of perjury at a trial, hearing, or other proceeding, or in a deposition. The rule as finally adopted covers statements before a grand jury. Prior inconsistent statements, the Conference Committee report points out, may of course be used for impeaching the credibility of a witness. When the prior inconsistent statement is one made by a defendant in a criminal case, it is covered by Rule 801 (d) (2).

Additionally, as submitted by the Supreme Court and passed by the House, subdivision (d) (1) (C) made admissible a prior statement identifying a person the witness had perceived. The Conference Committee decided to delete this provision because of its concern that a person could be convicted solely upon evidence admissible under this particular subdivision.

With respect to admissions covered by subdivision (d) (2), the Advisory Committee explained that this exclusion from the category of hearsay is based on the theory that the admissibility of admissions is the result of the adversary system rather than satisfaction of conditions of the hearsay rule. The freedom of admissions from technical demands searching for assurance of trustworthiness in some against-interest circumstances and from the restrictive influences of the opinion rule and the rule requiring firsthand knowledge, when taken with the apparently prevalent satisfaction with the results, calls for generous treatment of this avenue to admissibility. The rule specifies five categories of statements for which the responsibility of a party is considered sufficient to justify reception of evidence against him. With respect to the last of these five categories—a statement by a co-conspirator of a party during the course of and in furtherance of the conspiracy—the report of the Senate Committee indicated that the Committee understood the rule to carry forward the universally accepted doctrine that a joint venturer is considered a co-conspirator for the purpose of the rule even though no conspiracy has been charged.

Rule 802. Hearsay Rule

Hearsay is not admissible except as provided by these rules or by other rules prescribed by the Supreme Court pursuant to statutory authority or by Act of Congress.

COMMENT: This rule was enacted by Congress in substantially the same form submitted by the Court. Congress substituted the word "prescribed" in place of "adopted" and inserted the phrase "pursuant to statutory authority."

The Advisory Committee explained that this provision excepts from the operation of the rule hearsay made admissible by other rules. Some examples listed by the Advisory Committee to illustrate the working of the exception include FED. R. CIV. P. 4 (g) , 32, 43 (e) , 56, and 65 (b) ; FED. R. CRIM. P. 4 (a) , 12 (b) (4) ; 10 U.S.C. § 7730; 29 U.S.C. § 161 (4) ; and 38 U.S.C. § 5206.

Rule 803. Hearsay Exceptions; Availability of Declarant Immaterial

The following are not excluded by the hearsay rule, even though the declarant is available as a witness:

(1) **Present sense impression.** A statement describing or explaining an event or condition made while the declarant was perceiving the event or condition, or immediately thereafter.

(2) **Excited utterance.** A statement relating to a startling

event or condition made while the declarant was under the stress of excitement caused by the event or condition.

(3) **Then existing mental, emotional, or physical condition.** A statement of the declarant's then existing state of mind, emotion, sensation, or physical condition (such as intent, plan, motive, design, mental feeling, pain, and bodily health), but not including a statement of memory or belief to prove the fact remembered or believed unless it relates to the execution, revocation, identification, or terms of declarant's will.

(4) **Statements for purposes of medical diagnosis or treatment.** Statements made for purposes of medical diagnosis or treatment and describing medical history, or past or present symptoms, pain, or sensations, or the inception or general character of the cause or external source thereof insofar as reasonably pertinent to diagnosis or treatment.

(5) **Recorded recollection.** A memorandum or record concerning a matter about which a witness once had knowledge but now has insufficient recollection to enable him to testify fully and accurately, shown to have been made or adopted by the witness when the matter was fresh in his memory and to reflect that knowledge correctly. If admitted, the memorandum or record may be read into evidence but may not itself be received as an exhibit unless offered by an adverse party.

(6) **Records of regularly conducted activity.** A memorandum, report, record, or data compilation, in any form, of acts, events, conditions, opinions, or diagnoses, made at or near the time by, or from information transmitted by, a person with knowledge, if kept in the course of a regularly conducted business activity, and if it was the regular practice of that business activity to make the memorandum, report, record, or data compilation, all as shown by the testimony of the custodian or other qualified witness, unless the source of information or the method or circumstances of preparation indicate lack of trustworthiness. The term "business" as used in this paragraph includes business, institution, association, profession, occupation, and calling of every kind, whether or not conducted for profit.

(7) **Absence of entry in records kept in accordance with the provisions of paragraph (6).** Evidence that a matter is not included in the memoranda, reports, records, or data compilations, in any form, kept in accordance with the provisions of paragraph (6), to prove the nonoccurrence or nonexistence of

the matter, if the matter was of a kind of which a memorandum, report, record, or data compilation was regularly made and preserved, unless the sources of information or other circumstances indicate lack of trustworthiness.

(8) Public records and reports. Records, reports, statements, or data compilations, in any form, of public offices or agencies, setting forth (A) the activities of the office or agency, or (B) matters observed pursuant to duty imposed by law as to which matters there was a duty to report, excluding, however, in criminal cases matters observed by police officers and other law enforcement personnel, or (C) in civil actions and proceedings and against the Government in criminal cases, factual findings resulting from an investigation made pursuant to authority granted by law, unless the sources of information or other circumstances indicate lack of trustworthiness.

(9) Records of vital statistics. Records or data compilations, in any form, of births, fetal deaths, deaths, or marriages, if the report thereof was made to a public office pursuant to requirements of law.

(10) Absence of public record or entry. To prove the absence of a record, report, statement, or data compilation, in any form, or the nonoccurrence or nonexistence of a matter of which a record, report, statement, or data compilation, in any form, was regularly made and preserved by a public office or agency, evidence in the form of a certification in accordance with rule 902, or testimony, that diligent search failed to disclose the record, report, statement, or data compilation, or entry.

(11) Records of religious organizations. Statements of births, marriages, divorces, deaths, legitimacy, ancestry, relationship by blood or marriage, or other similar facts of personal or family history, contained in a regularly kept record of a religious organization.

(12) Marriage, baptismal, and similar certificates. Statements of fact contained in a certificate that the maker performed a marriage or other ceremony or administered a sacrament, made by a clergyman, public official, or other person authorized by the rules or practices of a religious organization or by law to perform the act certified, and purporting to have been issued at the time of the act or within a reasonable time thereafter.

(13) Family records. Statements of fact concerning personal or family history contained in family Bibles, genealogies, charts, engravings on rings, inscriptions on family portraits, engravings on urns, crypts, or tombstones, or the like.

(14) **Records of documents affecting an interest in property.** The record of a document purporting to establish or affect an interest in property, as proof of the content of the original recorded document and its execution and delivery by each person by whom it purports to have been executed, if the record is a record of a public office and an applicable statute authorizes the recording of documents of that kind in that office.

(15) **Statements in documents affecting an interest in property.** A statement contained in a document purporting to establish or affect an interest in property if the matter stated was relevant to the purpose of the document, unless dealings with the property since the document was made have been inconsistent with the truth of the statement or the purport of the document.

(16) **Statements in ancient documents.** Statements in a document in existence twenty years or more the authenticity of which is established.

(17) **Market reports, commercial publications.** Market quotations, tabulations, lists, directories, or other published compilations, generally used and relied upon by the public or by persons in particular occupations.

(18) **Learned treatises.** To the extent called to the attention of an expert witness upon cross-examination or relied upon by him in direct examination, statements contained in published treatises, periodicals, or pamphlets on a subject of history, medicine, or other science or art, established as a reliable authority by the testimony or admission of the witness or by other expert testimony or by judicial notice. If admitted, the statements may be read into evidence but may not be received as exhibits.

(19) **Reputation concerning personal or family history.** Reputation among members of his family by blood, adoption, or marriage, or among his associates, or in the community, concerning a person's birth, adoption, marriage, divorce, death, legitimacy, or relationship by blood, adoption, or marriage, ancestry, or other similar fact of his personal or family history.

(20) **Reputation concerning boundaries or general history.** Reputation in a community, arising before the controversy, as to boundaries of or customs affecting lands in the community,

and reputation as to events of general history important to the community or State or nation in which located.

(21) Reputation as to character. Reputation of a person's character among his associates or in the community.

(22) Judgment of previous conviction. Evidence of a final judgment, entered after trial or upon a plea of guilty (but not upon a plea of nolo contendere), adjudging a person guilty of a crime punishable by death or imprisonment in excess of one year, to prove any fact essential to sustain the judgment, but not including, when offered by the Government in a criminal prosecution for purposes other than impeachment, judgments against persons other than the accused. The pendency of an appeal may be shown but does not affect admissibility.

(23) Judgment as to personal, family or general history, or boundaries. Judgments as proof of matters of personal, family or general history, or boundaries, essential to the judgment, if the same would be provable by evidence of reputation.

(24) Other exceptions. A statement not specifically covered by any of the foregoing exceptions but having equivalent circumstantial guarantees of trustworthiness, if the court determines that (A) the statement is offered as evidence of a material fact; (B) the statement is more probative on the point for which it is offered than any other evidence which the proponent can procure through reasonable efforts; and (C) the general purposes of these rules and the interests of justice will best be served by admission of the statement into evidence. However, a statement may not be admitted under this exception unless the proponent of it makes known to the adverse party sufficiently in advance of the trial or hearing to provide the adverse party with a fair opportunity to prepare to meet it, his intention to offer the statement and the particulars of it, including the name and address of the declarant.

COMMENT: Congress, in adopting this rule, retained all 24 exceptions set forth in the rule as submitted by the Court. However, exceptions (6), (8), and (24) were substantially changed. Exceptions (5), (7), (14), and (16) were amended in minor fashion. All other exceptions were adopted as submitted.

The Advisory Committee pointed out that all the exceptions are phrased in terms of nonapplication of the hearsay rule rather than in positive terms of admissibility, in order to repel any implication that other possible grounds for exclusion are eliminated from consideration.

Exceptions (1) and (2) were adopted as submitted by the Court. The Advisory Committee noted that these two exceptions overlap in considerable measure even though they are based on somewhat different theories.

The underlying theory of exception (1) is that contemporaneity of event and statement negative the likelihood of deliberate or conscious misrepresentation. Exception (2) is based on the theory that circumstances may produce a condition of excitement which temporarily stills the capacity of reflection and produces utterances free of conscious fabrication. Spontaneity is the key factor in each instance, though arrived at by somewhat different routes. Both are needed to avoid needless niggling.

Permissible subject matter of the statement is limited under exception (1) to description or explanation of the event or condition, the assumption being that spontaneity, in the absence of a startling event, may extend no further. In exception (2), however, the statement need only relate to the startling event or condition, thus affording a broader scope of subject-matter coverage.

Exception (3), which was also adopted as submitted by the Court, is essentially a specialized application of exception (1), presented separately to enhance its usefulness and accessibility. The "but not" clause is essential, the Advisory Committee stresses, to avoid the virtual destruction of the hearsay rule that would otherwise result from allowing state of mind, provable by hearsay satement, to serve as the basis for an inference of the happening of the event which produced the state of mind. The rule does permit allowing evidence of intention as tending to prove the doing of the act intended.

While the House Committee approved exception (3) in the form submitted by the Court, it did so with the understanding that the rule would be construed to limit evidence of intention so as to render statements of intent by a declarant admissible only to prove his future conduct, not the future conduct of another person.

Exception (4), which was adopted as submitted by the Court, discards, the Advisory Committee emphasized, the conventional distinction between excluding from the hearsay exception statements to a physician consulted only for the purpose of enabling him to testify and the allowance of experts to state the basis of their opinion. This position, the Committee points out, is consistent with the provision of Rule 703 that the facts on which an expert's testimony is based need not be admissible in evidence if of a kind ordinarily relied upon by experts in the field. Exception (4) also extends, in accord with the current trend, to statements as to causation reasonably pertinent to the purposes of diagnosis or a treatment.

The House Committee, though it approved the rule as submitted by the Court, did so with the understanding that the exception is not intended in any way to adversely effect present privilege rules or those subsequently adopted. The Senate Committee Report expressed a similar view and pointed out that exception (4) must also be read in conjunction with FED. R. CIV. P. 35, which provides that whenever the physical or the mental condition of a party is in controversy, the court may require him to submit to an examination by a physician. It is these examinations, the report continued, which will normally be admitted under this exception.

Exception (5) as submitted by the Court permitted the reading into evidence of a memorandum or a record concerning a matter about which the witness once had knowledge but later had insufficient recollection to enable him to testify accurately and fully, "shown to have been made when the matter was fresh in his memory and to reflect that knowledge correctly." The House amended the rule to add the words "or adopted by the witness" after the phrase "shown to have been made," language parallel to the Jencks Act, 18 U.S.C. § 3500. The Senate Committee accepted the House amendment with the understanding that it was not intended to narrow the scope of applicability of the rule. Rather, the Committee understood it to clarify the rule's applicability to a memorandum adopted by the witness as well as the one made by him. The Senate Committee viewed the House amendment as a helpful clarification, observing, however, that the Advisory Committee note to the rule suggests that the important thing is the accuracy of the memorandum rather than who made it. Nor did the Senate Committee view the House amendment as precluding admissibility in situations in which multiple participants were involved. When the verifying witness has not prepared the report, but merely has examined it and found it accurate, he has adopted the report, and it is therefore admissible. The rule, the Committee continued, should also be interpreted to cover other situations involving multiple participants, e.g., employer dictating to secretary, secretary making memorandum at direction of employer, or information being passed along the chain of persons.

The Senate Committee also accepted the understanding of the House that a memorandum or report, although barred under this rule, would nonetheless be admissible if it came within another hearsay exception and noted that it considered this principle to be applicable to all the hearsay rules.

Exception (6) as submitted by the Court permitted a record made "in the course of a regularly conducted activity" to be admissible in certain circumstances. The House Committee, believing there were insufficient guarantees of reliability in records made in the course of activities falling outside the scope of "business" activities, concluded that the additional requirements of 28 U.S.C. § 1732 that it must have been the regular practice of a business to make the record is a necessary assurance of its trustworthiness. The Committee amended the rule to incorporate the limitations of Section 1732.

The Senate Committee disagreed. Even under the House definition of "business" including profession, occupation, and "calling of every kind," the Senate Committee report notes, the records of many regularly conducted activities will, or may be, excluded from evidence. The records of many institutions or groups might not be admissible under the House amendments. Therefore, the Senate Committee deleted the word "business" as it appears before the word "activity." The last sentence was thus rendered unnecessary and was also deleted.

The Conference Committee adopted the House provision that the records must be those for regularly conducted "business" activity. However, the conferees changed the definition of "business" contained in the House provision in order to make it clear that the records of institutions and associations, like those of schools, churches, and hospitals, are admissible under the provisions. The records of public schools and hospitals, the Conference Committee report emphasized, are also covered by Rule 803 (8) , which deals with public records and reports.

The Advisory Committee note to exception (6) states that the form which the record may assume under the rule is described broadly as a memorandum, report, record, or data compilation, in any form. The expression "data compilation" is used as broadly descriptive of any means of storing information other than the conventional words and figures in written documentary form. According to the Committee, it includes, but is by no means limited to, electronic computer storage. The term is borrowed from revised FED. R. CIV. P. 34 (a) .

Exception (7) as submitted by the Court concerned the absence of entry in the records of a "regularly conducted activity." In Congress this exception was amended to conform with the action taken with respect to exception (6). The Advisory Committee, in its note to exception (7) , pointed out that the failure of a record to mention a matter that ordinarily would be mentioned is satisfactory evidence of its nonexistence. While probably not hearsay as defined in Rule 801, decisions may be found, the Committee explained, which class the evidence not only as hearsay but also as not within any exception. In order to set the question at rest in favor of admissibility, the matter is specifically treated by exception (7) .

Exception (8) was substantially changed in the House. The House Committee approved the rule without substantive change, noting only that it intended the phrase "factual findings" to be strictly construed and that evaluations or opinions contained in public reports be inadmissible under this exception. However, before passage by the House, amendments offered on the floor by Congresswoman Holtzman (D-NY) and Congressman Dennis (R-Ind) were adopted. The amendment introduced by the former was intended to make it crystal clear that random observations by a government employee could not be introduced as exceptions to the hearsay rule and be insulated from cross-examination. The amendment restricted the exception to reports of "matters observed" by a public official only if the public official had a duty to report about such matters. The second amendment excluded from this exception matters observed by the police officers and other law enforcement personnel in criminal cases. The Senate Committee unsuccessfully recommended that the latter amendment include a reference to Rule 804 (b) (5), which allows the admission of such reports, records, or other statements where the police officer or other law enforcement officer was unavailable because of death, then-existing physical or mental illness or infirmity, or not being subject to legal process. This version of Rule 804 (b) (5) was not included in the rules as enacted. The Senate Committee also differed over the House Committee's construction of "factual findings." The Senate Committee called attention to the Advisory Committee notes on subsection (C) of exception (8), which pointed out that various kinds of evaluative reports are now admissible under federal statutes. These statutory exceptions to the hearsay rule are preserved. See Rule 802. The willingness of Congress to recognize these and other such evaluative reports provides a helpful guide in determining the kinds of reports which are intended to be admissible under this rule. The restrictive interpretation of the House Committee, the Senate Committee observed, overlooks the fact that while the Advisory Committee assumes admissibility in the first instance of evaluative reports, they are not admissible if as the rule states, "the sources of information or other circumstances indicate lack of trustworthiness."

The Advisory Committee specified several factors that may be of assistance in passing upon the admissibility of evaluative reports. These included: (1) the timeliness of the investigation; (2) the special skill or experience of the official; (3) whether a hearing was held in the level at which conducted; and (4) possible motivation problems suggested by *Palmer* v. *Hoffman,* 318 U.S. 109 (1943).

Exception (9), according to the Advisory Committee, is in principle narrower than Uniform Rule 63 (16), which includes reports required of persons performing functions authorized by statute, but is in practical effect substantially the same. Exception (10), the Advisory Committee explains, extends the principle of proving non-occurrence developed in exception (7) to public records of the kind mentioned in exceptions (8) and (9). The exception includes situations in which absence of a record may itself be the ultimate focal point of inquiry, e.g., a certificate of a Secretary of State admitted to show a failure to file documents required by state securities law. The Advisory Committee was of the view that the refusal of the common law to allow proof by certificate of the lack of a record or entry had no apparent justification.

With respect to exception (11) the Advisory Committee explained that records of activities of religious organizations are currently recognized as admissible at least to the extent of the business-records exception to the hearsay rule and that exception (6) would be applicable. However, the Committee continued, both the business-record doctrine and exception (6) require that the person furnishing the information be one in the business or activity. Exception (11) contains no requirement that the informant be in the course of the activity.

Exception (12), the Advisory Committee explained, extends the certification procedure found in exceptions (8) and (10) to clergymen and the like who perform marriages and other ceremonies or administer sacraments. However, when the person executing the certificate is not a public official, the self-authenticating character of documents purporting to emanate from public officials [see Rule 902] is lacking, and proof is required that the person was authorized and did make the certificate. The time element, however, may safely be taken as supplied by the certificate, once authority and authenticity are established.

While the House Committee accepted exception (13) as submitted, it did note its intention that the phrase "statements of fact concerning personal or family history" be read to include the specific types of statements enumerated in Rule 803 (11).

With respect to exception (14) the Advisory Committee pointed out that the recording of title documents is a purely statutory development. The Advisory Committee further noted that what may appear in the rule, at first glance, as endowing the record with an effect independent of local law and inviting difficulties of an *Erie* nature under *City Service Oil Co.* v. *Dunlap,* 308 U.S. 208 (1939), is not present, since the local law in fact governs under the example.

Concerning exception (15), the Advisory Committee said that the circumstances under which dispositive documents are executed and the requirement that the recital be germane to the purpose of the document are adequate guarantees of trustworthiness, particularly in view of the nonapplicability of the rule if dealings with the property have been inconsistent with the document.

With respect to exception (16), the Advisory Committee explained that most ancient documents are significant evidentially only insofar as they are assertive, and that therefore their admission in evidence must be as a hearsay exception. Danger of mistake is minimized, the Committee continued, by authentication requirements, and age affords assurance that the writing antedates the existing controversy.

The Advisory Committee found ample authority at common law to support the admission of items falling in the category embraced by exception (17). The basis of trustworthiness is generally reliance by the public or by a particular segment of it, and the motivation of the compiler to force the reliance by being accurate.

With respect to exception (18) the Advisory Committee explained that while "the writers have generally favored the admissibility of learned treatises," the great weight of authority has been that learned treatises are not admissible as substantive evidence, though usable in the cross-examination of experts. The rule avoids the danger of misunderstanding and misapplication by limiting the use of treatises as substantive evidence to situations in which an expert is on the stand and available to explain and assist in the application of the treatise if desired. The limitation upon receiving the publication itself physically in evidence, contained in the last sentence, is designed to further this policy. Exception (18) does not require that the witness rely upon a recognized treatise as authoritative, thus avoiding the possibility that the expert may at the outset block cross-examination by refusing to concede reliance or authoritativeness. Moreover, this exception avoids the unreality of admitting evidence for the purpose of impeachment only, with an instruction to the jury not to consider it otherwise. The parallel to the treatment of prior inconsistent statements is apparent. [See Rule 801 (d) (1) .]

Exception (19), is concerned with matters of personal and family history. Marriage is universally conceded to be a proper subject of proof by evidence of reputation in the community. Items such as legitimacy, relationship, adoption, birth, and death have been treated in diverse ways by the decisions, the Advisory Committee concluded.

The first portion of exception (20), the Advisory Committee explained, is based upon the general admissibility of evidence of reputation as to land boundaries and land customs, expanded in this country to include private as well as public boundaries. The second portion is likewise supported by authority and is designed to facilitate proof of events when judicial notice is not available. The historical character of the subject matter dispenses with any need that the reputation antedate the controversy with respect to which it is offered.

Exception (21), the Advisory Committee noted, recognizes the traditional acceptance of reputation evidence as a means of proving human character. The exception deals only with the hearsay aspect of this kind of evidence. Limitations upon admissibility based on other grounds are found in Rules 404 and 608.

Exception (22), the Advisory Committee observed, does not deal with the substantive effect of a judgment as a bar or collateral estoppel. The exception adopts the theory that, when the doctrine of res judicata does not apply to make the judgment either a bar or a collateral estoppel, judgments of criminal conviction of felony grade are admissible in evidence for what they are worth. This is the direction of the decisions. Practical considerations require exclusion of evidence of convictions of minor offenses because motivation to defend at this level is often minimal or nonexistent. Judgments of conviction based upon pleas of nolo contendere are not included. This position is consistent with the treatment of nolo pleas in Rule 410.

The Advisory Committee note to exception (23) illustrates the range of matters provable by judgment as to personal, family, or general history, or boundaries. *Patterson* v. *Gaines,* 47 U.S. 550 (1847), followed in the pattern of the English decisions, mentioning as provable matters manorial rights, public rights of way, immemorial custom, disputed boundary, and pedigree. More recent cases have recognized, among others, a decision of a board of inquiry of the immigration service as admissible to prove alienage of laborers, and records of a commission enrolling Indians, both as admissible on pedigree, and immigration board decisions as to the citizenship of the plaintiff's father as admissible in a proceeding for declaration of citizenship.

Exception (24) went through several changes in the Congress. As submitted to Congress, it contained a provision to the effect that the federal courts could admit any hearsay statement not specifically covered by any of the stated exceptions, if the hearsay statement was found to have "comparable circumstantial guarantees of truthworthiness." The House Committee deleted this provision as injecting too much uncertainty into the law of evidence and impairing the ability of practitioners to prepare for trial. The House Committee believed that if additional hearsay exceptions are to be created, they should be by amendments to the rules, not on a case-by-case basis. The Senate disagreed with the deletion and added a new exception (24), which made admissible a hearsay statement not specifically covered by any of the previous 23 exceptions if the statement had "equivalent" circumstantial guarantees of trustworthiness and if the court determined that (A) the statement was offered as evidence of a material fact; (B) the statement was more probative on the point for which it was offered than any other evidence the proponent could procure through reasonable efforts; and (C) the general purposes of these rules and the interests of justice would be best served by admission of the statement into evidence.

The Conference Committee adopted the Senate amendment with an amendment providing that a party intending to request the court to use a statement under this provision must notify any adverse party of this intention as well as of the particulars of the statement, including the name and address of the declarant. This notice must be given sufficiently in advance of the trial or hearing to provide any adverse party with the fair opportunity to prepare to contest the use of this statement.

Rule 804. Hearsay Exceptions: Declarant Unavailable

(a) **Definition of unavailability.** "Unavailability as a witness" includes situations in which the declarant—

(1) is exempted by ruling of the court on the ground of privilege from testifying concerning the subject matter of his statement; or

(2) persists in refusing to testify concerning the subject matter of his statement despite an order of the court to do so; or

(3) testifies to a lack of memory of the subject matter of his statement; or

(4) is unable to be present or to testify at the hearing because of death or then existing physical or mental illness or infirmity; or

(5) is absent from the hearing and the proponent of his statement has been unable to procure his attendance (or in the case of a hearsay exception under subdivision (b) (2), (3), or (4), his attendance or testimony) by process or other reasonable means.

A declarant is not unavailable as a witness if his exemption, refusal, claim of lack of memory, inability, or absence is due to the procurement or wrongdoing of the proponent of his statement for the purpose of preventing the witness from attending or testifying.

(b) Hearsay exceptions. The following are not excluded by the hearsay rule if the declarant is unavailable as a witness:

(1) Former testimony. Testimony given as a witness at another hearing of the same or a different proceeding, or in a deposition taken in compliance with law in the course of the same or another proceeding, if the party against whom the testimony is now offered, or, in a civil action or proceeding, a predecessor in interest, had an opportunity and similar motive to develop the testimony by direct, cross, or redirect examination.

(2) Statement under belief of impending death. In a prosecution for homicide or in a civil action or proceeding, a statement made by a declarant while believing that his death was imminent, concerning the cause or circumstances of what he believed to be his impending death.

(3) Statement against interest. A statement which was at the time of its making so far contrary to the declarant's pecuniary or proprietary interest, or so far tended to subject him to civil or criminal liability, or to render invalid a claim by him against another, that a reasonable man in his position would not have made the statement unless he believed it to be true. A statement tending to expose the declarant to criminal liability and offered to exculpate the accused is not admissible unless corroborating circumstances clearly indicate the trustworthiness of the statement.

(4) **Statement of personal or family history.** (A) A statement concerning the declarant's own birth, adoption, marriage, divorce, legitimacy, relationship by blood, adoption, or marriage, ancestry, or other similar fact of personal or family history, even though declarant had no means of acquiring personal knowledge of the matter stated; or (B) a statement concerning the foregoing matters, and death also, of another person, if the declarant was related to the other by blood, adoption, or marriage or was so intimately associated with the other's family as to be likely to have accurate information concerning the matter declared.

(5) **Other exceptions.** A statement not specifically covered by any of the foregoing exceptions but having equivalent circumstantial guarantees of trustworthiness, if the court determines that (A) the statement is offered as evidence of a material fact; (B) the statement is more probative on the point for which it is offered than any other evidence which the proponent can procure through reasonable efforts; and (C) the general purposes of these rules and the interests of justice will best be served by admission of the statement into evidence. However, a statement may not be admitted under this exception unless the proponent of it makes known to the adverse party sufficiently in advance of the trial or hearing to provide the adverse party with a fair opportunity to prepare to meet it, his intention to offer the statement and the particulars of it, including the name and address of the declarant.

COMMENT: This rule was amended in several respects by the Congress.

Subdivision (a) was adopted essentially as submitted by the Supreme Court. The Advisory Committee noted in regard to this subdivision that the definition of unavailability implements the division of hearsay exceptions into two categories by Rules 803 and 804 (b). At common law, the Advisory Committee explained, the unavailability requirement was evolved in connection with particular hearsay exceptions rather than along general lines. No reason is apparent for making distinctions as to what satisfies unavailability for the different exceptions. Therefore, the treatment in the rule is uniform although differences in the range of process for witnesses between civil and criminal cases will lead to less exacting requirements under item (5). [See FED. R. CIV. P. 45 (e) and FED. R. CRIM. P. 17 (e).]

With respect to Rule 804 (a) (3), the House Committee stated that no change was intended in existing federal law under which a court may choose to disbelieve the declarant's testimony as to his lack of memory. The House Committee did amend Rule 804 (a) (5) to require that an attempt be made to depose a witness, as well as to seek his attendance, as a precondition to the witness being unavailable. Under this amendment, before a witness is declared unavailable, a party must try to depose of a witness with respect to dying declarations, declarations against interests, and declarations of pedigree. The Senate Committee felt that none of these situations "warrant this needless, impractical and highly restrictive complication." The Senate Committee also stated its understanding that the rule as to unavailability as explained by the Advisory Committee contained no requirement that an attempt be made to take a deposition of a declarant. Although the Senate deleted the House amendment, it was adopted by the Conference Committee.

Rule 804 (b) (1) as submitted by the Court allowed prior testimony of an unavailable witness to be deemed admissible if the party against whom it was offered or a person "with motive and interest similar" to his had an opportunity to examine the witness. The House Committee considered that it was generally unfair to impose upon the party against whom the hearsay evidence was being offered responsibility for the manner in which the witness was previously handled by another party. The sole exception to this in the Committee's view was when a party's predecessor in interest in a civil action or a proceeding had an opportunity and similar motive to examine the witness. The rule was amended to reflect these views.

Exception (2) as submitted by the Supreme Court dealt with statements of recent perception and was deleted by the Congress. Rule 804 (b) (2) as enacted by Congress is exception (3) as submitted by the Court. This exception is the familiar dying declaration of the common law, expanded somewhat beyond its traditionally narrow limits. As submitted by the Court, this exception would have allowed dying declarations in all criminal and civil cases. The House Committee did not consider dying declarations as among the most reliable forms of hearsay. Consequently, it amended the provision to limit admissibility in criminal cases to homicide prosecutions, where exceptional need for the evidence is present. This is existing law. At the same time, the Committee approved the expansion to civil actions and proceedings where the stakes do not involve possible imprisonment, although noting that this could lead to forum shopping in some instances.

Exception (3) as adopted by the Congress encompasses the statement against interest exception that constituted exception (4) as submitted by the Court. The Advisory Committee note to this section indicated that the common law required that the interest declared against be pecuniary or proprietary but that within this limitation the common law demonstrated a striking ingenuity in discovering an against-interest aspect. The exception discards the common law limitation and reaches its full logical limit. In accordance with the trend of the decisions in this country, one result is to remove doubt as to the admissibility of declarations tending to establish a tort liability against the declarant or to extinguish one which might be asserted by him. And finally, exposure to criminal liability satisfies the against-interest requirement of the exception. The House Committee made several changes in this exception as submitted by the Court. It agreed to retention of the traditional hearsay exception for statements against pecuniary or proprietary interest but deemed the submitted exception's additional references to statements tending to subject the declarant to civil liability or to render invalid a claim by him against another to be redundant as included within the scope of the reference to statements against pecuniary or proprietary interest. It also objected to the proposed exception's expansion of the hearsay limitation to include statements subjecting a declarant to criminal liability and statements tending to make him an object of hatred, ridicule, or disgrace. The House Committee eliminated the latter category from the subdivision as lacking sufficient guarantees of reliability. As for statements against penal interests, the House Committee shared the view of the Court that some such statements do possess adequate assurances of reliability that should be admissible. It believed, however, as did the Court, that statements of this type tending to exculpate the accused are more suspect and so should have their admissibility conditioned upon some further provision ensuring trustworthiness. The proposed requirement of simple corroboration was, however, deemed ineffective to accomplish this purpose. The House Committee settled upon the language "unless corroborating circumstances clearly indicate that the trustworthiness of the statement" as affording a proper standard and degree of discretion.

The Senate Committee, believing that the reference to statements tending to subject a person to civil liability constitute a desirable clarification of the scope of the rule, reinstated the Supreme Court language in this matter. It accepted the House Committee's elimination of the proposed inclusion of statements subjecting the declarant to statements tending to make him an object of hatred, ridicule, or disgrace. The Senate Committee also decided to delete the House amendment that would have codified the constitutional principle announced in *Bruton* v. *U.S.*, 391 U.S. 123 (1968), with respect to statements or confessions by co-defendants. The Senate Committee cited the basic approach of the rules in avoiding codification or attempted codification of constitutional evidentiary principles, such as the fifth-amendment right against self-incrimination and, here, the sixth-amendment right of confrontation.

Moreover, the Senate Committee did not feel that the House provision properly recognized the exceptions to the *Bruton* rule. The Conference Committee adopted the Senate amendment. The conferees specified their intention to include within the purview of the rule statements subjecting a person to civil liability and statements rendering claims invalid.

Exception (4) as submitted by the Court was amended by the Conference Committee in conformity with the views it expressed with respect to its amendment of Rule 803 (24), above.

The Senate had added a new hearsay exception, not contained in the House bill, which would have provided that certain law enforcement records are admissible if the officer-declarant is unavailable to testify or to be present because of (1) death or physical or mental illness or infirmity or (2) absence from the proceeding, if the proponent of the statement had been unable to procure his attendance by process or other reasonable means. This amendment was not adopted by the Conference Committee.

Rule 805. Hearsay Within Hearsay

Hearsay included within hearsay is not excluded under the hearsay rule if each party of the combined statements conforms with an exception to the hearsay rule provided in these rules.

COMMENT: This rule was enacted by Congress as submitted by the Court.

The Advisory Committee cited the following illustration of how this rule would operate. A hospital record might contain an entry of the patient's age based on information furnished by his wife. The hospital record would qualify as a regular entry except that the person who furnished the information was not acting in the routine of the business. However, her statement independently qualifies as a statement of pedigree (if she is unavailable) or as a statement made for the purposes of diagnosis or treatment, and hence each link in the chain falls under sufficient assurances. Similarly, a dying declaration may incorporate a declaration against interest by another declarant.

Rule 806. Attacking and Supporting Credibility of Declarant

When a hearsay statement, or a statement defined in Rule 801 (d) (2), (C), (D), or (E), has been admitted in evidence, the credibility of the declarant may be attacked, and if attacked may be supported, by any evidence which would be admissible for those purposes if declarant had testified as a witness. Evidence of a statement or conduct by the declarant at any time, inconsistent with his hearsay statement, is not subject to any requirement that he may have been afforded an opportunity to deny or explain. If the party against whom a hearsay statement has been admitted calls the declarant as a witness, the party is entitled to examine him on the statement as if under cross-examination.

COMMENT: This rule was adopted by Congress with an amendment to bring within the rule's scope statements defined in Rule 801 (d) (2), (C), (D), or (E). The Senate Committee explained that, as proposed by the Court, whenever a hearsay statement is admitted, the credibility of the declarant of the statement may be attacked, and, if attacked, may be supported by any evidence that would be admissible for those purposes if the defendant had testified as a witness. Rule 801 defines what a hearsay statement is. While statements by a party authorized by a party opponent to make a statement concerning the subject, by the party-opponent's agent, or by a co-conspirator of a party [see Rule 801 (d) (2) (C), (D), and (E)] traditionally are defined as exceptions to the hearsay rule, Rule 801 defines such admissions by a party opponent as statements that are not hearsay. Consequently, Rule 806, by referring exclusively to the admission of hearsay statements, does not appear to allow the credibility of the declarant to be attacked when the declarant is a co-conspirator, agent, or authorized spokesman. The Senate Committee was of the view that such statements should open the declarant to attacks on his credibility.

ARTICLE IX. AUTHENTICATION AND IDENTIFICATION

Rule 901. Requirement of Authentication or Identification

(a) **General provision.** The requirement of authentication or identification as a condition precedent to admissibility is satisfied by evidence sufficient to support a finding that the matter in question is what its proponent claims.

(b) **Illustrations.** By way of illustration only, and not by way of limitation, the following are examples of authentication or identification conforming with the requirements of this rule:

(1) **Testimony of witness with knowledge.** Testimony that a matter is what it is claimed to be.

(2) **Nonexpert opinion on handwriting.** Nonexpert opinion as to the genuineness of handwriting, based upon familiarity not acquired for purposes of the litigation.

(3) **Comparison by trier or expert witness.** Comparison by the trier of fact or by expert witnesses with specimens which have been authenticated.

(4) **Distinctive characteristics and the like.** Appearance, contents, substance, internal patterns, or other distinctive characteristics, taken in conjunction with circumstances.

(5) **Voice identification.** Identification of a voice, whether heard firsthand or through mechanical or electronic transmission or recording, by opinion based upon hearing the voice at any time under circumstances connecting it with the alleged speaker.

(6) **Telephone conversations.** Telephone conversations, by evidence that a call was made to the number assigned at the time by the telephone company to a particular person or business, if (A) in the case of a person, circumstances, including self-identification, show the person answering to be the one called, or (B) in the case of a business, the call was made to a place of business and the conversation related to business reasonably transacted over the telephone.

(7) **Public records or reports.** Evidence that a writing authorized by law to be recorded or filed and in fact recorded or filed in a public office, or a purported public record, report,

statement, or data compilation, in any form, is from the public office where items of this nature are kept.

(8) Ancient documents or data compilation. Evidence that a document or data compilation, in any form, (A) is in such condition as to create no suspicion concerning its authenticity, (B) was in place where it, if authentic, would likely be, and (C) has been in existence 20 years or more at the time it is offered.

(9) Process or system. Evidence describing a process or system used to produce a result and showing that the process or system produces an accurate result.

(10) Methods provided by statute or rule. Any method of authentication or identification provided by Act of Congress or by other rules prescribed by the Supreme Court pursuant to statutory authority.

COMMENT: This rule was enacted by Congress essentially as submitted to it by the Court. A minor amendment to subdivision (b) (10) substituted "prescribed" for "adopted," and added "pursuant to statutory authority."

The Advisory Committee explained that subdivision (a)'s requirement of showing authenticity or identity falls in the category of relevancy dependent upon fulfillment of a condition of fact and is governed by the procedure set forth in Rule 104 (b).

The treatment of authentication and identification under subdivision (b), the Advisory Committee observed, was based largely upon the experience embodied in the criminal law and in statutes in order to furnish illustrative applications of the general principles set forth in subdivision (a). The examples are not intended as an exclusive enumeration of allowable methods but are meant to guide and suggest, leaving room for growth and development in this area of the law. The Committee also said that compliance with requirements of authentication or identification does not assure admission of an item into evidence, in that other bars to its admission may remain.

Rule 902. Self-Authentication

Extrinsic evidence of authenticity as a condition precedent to admissibility is not required with respect to the following:

(1) Domestic public documents under seal. A document bearing a seal purporting to be that of the United States, or any State, district, Commonwealth, territory, or insular possession thereof, or the Panama Canal Zone, or the Trust Territory of the Pacific Islands, or of a political subdivision, department, officer, or agency thereof, and a signature purporting to be an attestation or execution.

(2) **Domestic public documents not under seal.** A document purporting to bear the signature in his official capacity of an officer or employee of any entity included in paragraph (1) hereof, having no seal, if a public officer having a seal and having official duties in the district or political subdivision of the officer or employee certifies under seal that the signer has the official capacity and that the signature is genuine.

(3) **Foreign public documents.** A document purporting to be executed or attested in his official capacity by a person authorized by the laws of a foreign country to make the execution or attestation, and accompanied by a final certification as to the genuineness of the signature and official position (A) of the executing or attesting person, or (B) of any foreign official whose certificate of genuineness of signature and official position relates to the execution or attestation or is in a chain of certificates of genuineness of signature and official position relating to the execution or attestation. A final certification may be made by a secretary of embassy or legation, consul general, consul, vice consul, or consular agent of the United States, or a diplomatic or consular official of the foreign country assigned or accredited to the United States. If reasonable opportunity has been given to all parties to investigate the authenticity and accuracy of official documents, the court may, for good cause shown, order that they be treated as presumptively authentic without final certification or permit them to be evidenced by an attested summary with or without final certification.

(4) **Certified copies of public records.** A copy of an official record or report or entry therein, or of a document authorized by law to be recorded or filed and actually recorded or filed in a public office, including data compilations in any form, certified as correct by the custodian or other person authorized to make the certification, by certificate complying with paragraph (1), (2), or (3) of this rule or complying with any Act of Congress or rule prescribed by the Supreme Court pursuant to statutory authority.

(5) **Official publications.** Books, pamphlets, or other publications purporting to be issued by public authority.

(6) Newspapers and periodicals. Printed materials purporting to be newspapers or periodicals.

(7) Trade inscriptions and the like. Inscriptions, signs, tags or labels purporting to have been affixed in the course of business and indicating ownership, control, or origin.

(8) Acknowledged documents. Documents accompanied by a certificate of acknowledgment exectuted in the manner provided by law by a notary public or other officer authorized by law to take acknowledgments.

(9) Commercial paper and related documents. Commercial paper, signatures thereon, and documents relating thereto to the extent provided by general commercial law.

(10) Presumptions under Acts of Congress. Any signature, document, or other matter declared by Act of Congress to be presumptively or prima facie genuine or authentic.

COMMENT: This rule was enacted essentially as submitted by the Court.

Paragraph (4) was amended by substituting "prescribed" for "adopted," and by adding "pursuant to statutory authority."

Paragraph (8) was amended by substituting "in the manner provided by law by" for "under the hand and seal of."

The Advisory Committee indicates that Rule 902 collects and incorporates the case law and statutes that have, over the years, developed a substantial body of instances in which authenticity is taken as sufficiently established for purposes of admissibility without extrinsic evidence to that effect. In some instances the rule does expand these situations to occupy a larger area, as justified by underlying considerations. In no instance, the Advisory Committee makes clear, is the opposite party foreclosed from disputing authenticity.

The change made by Congress in Rule 902 (8) was intended to eliminate the requirement, believed to be inconsistent with the law in some states, that a notary public must affix a seal to a document acknowledged before him. As amended the rule merely requires that the document be executed in the manner prescribed by state law.

Rule 903. Subscribing Witness' Testimony Unnecessary

The testimony of a subscribing witness is not necessary to authenticate a writing unless required by the laws of the jurisdiction whose laws govern the validity of the writing.

COMMENT: This rule was enacted by Congress as submitted by the Court.

The Advisory Committee note to this section explains that while common law required that an attesting witness be produced or accounted for, today the requirement has generally been abolished except with respect to documents that must be attested to be valid.

ARTICLE X. CONTENTS OF WRITINGS, RECORDINGS, AND PHOTOGRAPHS

Rule 1001. Definitions

For purposes of this article the following definitions are applicable:

(1) Writings and recordings. "Writings" and "recordings" consist of letters, words, or numbers, or their equivalent, set down by handwriting, typewriting, printing, photostating, photographing, magnetic impulse, mechanical or electronic recording, or other form of data compilation.

(2) Photographs. "Photographs" include still photographs, X-ray films, video tapes, and motion pictures.

(3) Original. An "original" of a writing or recording is the writing or recording itself or any counterpart intended to have the same effect by a person executing or issuing it. An "original" of a photograph includes the negative or any print therefrom. If data are stored in a computer or similar device, any printout or other output readable by sight, shown to reflect the data accurately, is an "original".

(4) Duplicate. A "duplicate" is a counterpart produced by the same impression as the original, or from the same matrix, or by means of photography, including enlargements and miniatures, or by mechanical or electronic re-recording, or by chemical reproduction, or by other equivalent techniques which accurately reproduces the original.

COMMENT: This rule was enacted by Congress as submitted by the Supreme Court, except that Congress added "videotapes" to the items treated as photographs in paragraph (2).

The Advisory Committee noted that in an earlier day the "best evidence" rule afforded substantial guarantees against inaccuracies and fraud. With the enlargement of discovery and related procedures, however, the need for the best-evidence rule has been measurably reduced. With respect to writings and recordings, the Committee took into account the fact that present-day techniques have expanded methods of storing data, and thus the rule necessarily has been expanded to include computers, photographic systems, and other modern developments. With respect to paragraph (3), the Committee explained that a contract executed in duplicate becomes an original, as does a sales-ticket carbon copy given to a customer. Paragraph (4) is intended to include within the definition of "copies" those produced by methods possessing an accuracy which virtually eliminates the possibility of error. Copies subsequently produced manually, whether handwritten or typed, are not within the definition. It should also be noted that what is an original for some purposes may be a duplicate for others. Thus, a bank's microfilm record of checks cleared is the original record. However, a print offered as a copy of a check whose contents are in controversy is a duplicate. This result is substantially consistent with 28 U.S.C. § 1732 (b).

Rule 1002. Requirement of Original

To prove the content of a writing, recording, or photograph, the original writing, recording, or photograph is required, except as otherwise provided in these rules or by Act of Congress.

COMMENT: This rule was enacted as submitted by the Court. The rule, the Advisory Committee commented, is the familiar one requiring production of the original of a document to prove its content, expanded to include writings, recordings, and photographs as defined in Rule 1001 (1) and (2). Application of the rule requires a resolution of the question whether the contents are sought to be proved. For example, payment may be proved without producing the written receipt given. Earnings may be proved without producing books of account in which they are entered. Nor does the rule apply to testimony that books or records have been examined and found not to contain any reference to the designated matter. The assumption should not be made that the rule will come into operation on every occasion when use is made of a photograph in evidence. On the contrary, the rule will seldom apply to ordinary photographs. In most instances a party wishes to introduce the item and the question raised is the propriety of receiving it in evidence. Cases in which an offer is made of the testimony of a witness as to what he saw in a photograph or a motion picture, without producing the same, are most unusual. The usual course is for a witness on the stand to identify the photograph or motion picture as a correct representation of events that he saw or of a scene with which he is familiar. Under these circumstances, no effort is made to prove the contents of the picture, and the rule is inapplicable.

Copyrights, defamation, and invasion of privacy by photograph or motion picture fall in the category of situations in which contents are sought to be proved.

It should also be noted that Rule 703 allows an expert to give an opinion based on matters not in evidence, and the present rule must be read as being limited accordingly in its application.

Rule 1003. Admissibility of Duplicates

A duplicate is admissible to the same extent as an original unless (1) a genuine question is raised as to the authenticity of the original or (2) in the circumstances it would be unfair to admit the duplicate in lieu of the original.

COMMENT: When the only concern is with getting the words or other contents before the court with accuracy and precision, a counterpart serves equally as well as the original, if the counterpart is the product of a method which insures accuracy and genuineness. By definition, the Advisory Committee continued, a "duplicate" under Rule 1001 (4) possesses this character. Therefore, if no genuine issue exists as to authenticity and no other reason exists for requiring the original, a duplicate is admissible under the rule.

Congress adopted this provision as submitted by the Court. The House Committee did so "with the expectation that the courts would be liberal in deciding that a 'genuine question is raised as to the authenticity of the original.' "

Rule 1004. Admissibility of Other Evidence of Contents

The original is not required, and other evidence of the contents of a writing, recording, or photograph is admissible if—

(1) **Originals lost or destroyed.** All originals are lost or have been destroyed, unless the proponent lost or destroyed them in bad faith; or

(2) **Original not obtainable.** No original can be obtained by any available judicial process or procedure; or

(3) **Original in possession of opponent.** At a time when an original was under the control of the party against whom offered, he was put on notice, by the pleadings or otherwise, that the contents would be a subject of proof at the hearing, and he does not produce the original at the hearing; or

(4) **Collateral matters.** The writing, recording, or photograph is not closely related to a controlling issue.

COMMENT: This rule was adopted as submitted by the Court. The Advisory Committee observed that, basically, the rule requiring the production of the original as proof of contents has developed as a rule of preference: If failure to produce the original is satisfactorily explained, secondary evidence is admissible. The instant rule specifies the circumstances under which production of the original is excused. The rule recognizes no "degrees" of secondary evidence.

With respect to Rule 1004 (1), the House Committee, while approving the language submitted by the Court, stated its intention that loss or destruction of an original by another person at the instigation of the proponent should be considered as tantamount to loss or destruction in bad faith by the proponent himself.

With respect to paragraph (2), the Advisory Committee indicated that when an original is in the possession of a third person, inability to procure it from him by resort to process or other judicial procedure is a sufficient explanation of nonproduction. Judicial procedure includes *subpoena duces tecum* as an incident to the taking of a deposition in another jurisdiction. The notice procedure provided in paragraph (3) is not to be confused with orders to produce or other discovery procedures, as the purpose of the procedure under this rule is to afford the opposite party an opportunity to produce the original, not to compel him to do so. The Committee also noted the difficulty of defining with precision, situations covered by paragraph (4) in which no good purpose is served by production of the original.

Rule 1005. Public Records

The contents of an official record, or of a document authorized to be recorded or filed and actually recorded or filed, including data compilations in any form, if otherwise admissible, may be proved by copy, certified as correct in accordance with rule 902 or testified to be correct by a witness who has compared it with the original. If a copy which complies with the foregoing cannot be obtained by the exercise of reasonable diligence, then other evidence of the contents may be given.

COMMENT: Congress enacted this rule as submitted to it by the Court.

While decisions and statutes have commonly held that no explanation need be given for failure to produce the original of a public record, the Advisory Committee believed that such blanket dispensation of producing or accounting for the original would open the door to the introduction of every kind of secondary evidence of contents of public records. The preference given certified or compared copies prevents this from happening. Recognition of "degrees" of secondary evidence in this situation is an appropriate *quid pro quo* for not requiring production of the original.

The rule applies to public records generally and is comparable in scope in this respect to FED. R. CIV. P. 44 (a).

Rule 1006. Summaries

The contents of voluminous writings, recordings, or photographs which cannot conveniently be examined in court may be presented in the form of a chart, summary, or calculation. The originals, or duplicates, shall be made available for examination or copying, or both, by other parties at reasonable time and place. The court may order that they be produced in court.

COMMENT: This rule was also enacted by Congress as submitted to it by the Court. The Advisory Committee observed that the admission of summaries of voluminous books, records, or documents offers the only practical means of making their contents available to judging jury. The rule merely recognizes this practice, with appropriate safeguards.

Rule 1007. Testimony or Written Admission of Party

Contents of writings, recordings, or photographs may be proved by the testimony or deposition of the party against whom offered or by his written admission, without accounting for the nonproduction of the original.

COMMENT: This rule was enacted by Congress as submitted to it by the Court. The instant rule, the Advisory Committee noted, follows Professor McCormick's suggestion of limiting this use of admissions to those made in the course of giving testimony or in writing. The limitation, of course, does not call for excluding evidence of an oral admission when nonproduction of the original has been accounted for and secondary evidence generally has become admissible. [See Rule 1004.]

Rule 1008. Functions of Court and Jury

When the admissibility of other evidence of contents of writings, recordings, or photographs under these rules depends upon the fulfillment of a condition of fact, the question whether the condition has been fulfilled is ordinarily for the court to determine in accordance with the provisions of rule 104. However, when an issue is raised (a) whether the asserted writing ever existed, or (b) whether another writing, recording, or photograph produced at the trial is the original, or (c) whether other evidence of contents correctly reflects the contents, the issue is for the trier of fact to determine as in the case of other issues of the fact.

COMMENT: This rule was enacted by Congress as submitted by the Court, with the exception that Congress added at the end of the first sentence the phrase "in accordance with the provisions of Rule 104."

The Advisory Committee note to the rule emphasized that most preliminary questions of fact in connection with applying the rule preferring the original as evidence of contents are for the judge under the general principles announced in Rule 104. Thus, the question of whether the loss of the originals has been established or of the fulfillment of other conditions specified in Rule 1004 is for the judge. However, questions may arise which go beyond the mere administration of the rule preferring the original and into the merits of the controversy. The latter portion of Rule 1008, the Advisory Committee indicated, is designed to insure treatment of these situations as raising jury questions. The decision is not one for the uncontrolled discretion of the jury but is subject to the control exercised generally by the judge over jury determinations.

ARTICLE XI. MISCELLANEOUS RULES

Rule 1101. Applicability of Rules

(a) **Courts and magistrates.** These rules apply to the United States district courts, the District Court of Guam, the District Court of the Virgin Islands, the District Court for the District of the Canal Zone, the United States courts of appeals, the Court of Claims, and to United States magistrates, in the actions, cases, and proceedings and to the extent hereinafter set forth. The terms "judge" and "court" in these rules include United States magistrates, referees in bankruptcy, and commissioners of the Court of Claims.

(b) **Proceedings generally.** These rules apply generally to civil actions and proceedings, including admiralty and maritime cases, to criminal cases and proceedings, to contempt proceedings except those in which the court may act summarily, and to proceedings and cases under the Bankruptcy Act.

(c) **Rule of privilege.** The rule with respect to privileges applies at all stages of all actions, cases, and proceedings.

(d) **Rules inapplicable.** The rules (other than with respect to privileges) do not apply in the following situations:

(1) **Preliminary questions of fact.** The determination of questions of fact preliminary to admissibility of evidence when the issue is to be determined by the court under rule 104.

(2) **Grand jury.** Proceedings before grand juries.

(3) **Miscellaneous proceedings.** Proceedings for extradition or rendition; preliminary examinations in criminal cases; sentencing, or granting or revoking probation; issuance of warrants for arrest, criminal summonses, and search warrants; and proceedings with respect to release on bail or otherwise.

(e) **Rules applicable in part.** In the following proceedings these rules apply to the extent that matters of evidence are not provided for in the statutes which govern procedure therein or in other rules prescribed by the Supreme Court pursuant to statutory authority: the trial of minor and petty offenses by United States magistrates; review of agency actions when the facts are subject to trial de novo under section 706 (2) (F) of title 5, United States Code;

90

review of orders of the Secretary of Agriculture under section 2 of the Act entitled "An Act to authorize association of producers of agricultural products" approved February 18, 1922 (7 U.S.C. 292), and under sections 6 and 7 (c) of the Perishable Agricultural Commodities Act, 1930 (7 U.S.C. 499f, 499g (c)) ; naturalization and revocation of naturalization under sections 310–318 of the Immigration and Nationality Act (8 U.S.C. 1421–1429) ; prize proceedings in admiralty under sections 7651–7681 of title 10, United States Code; review of orders of the Secretary of the Interior under section 2 of the Act entitled "An Act authorizing associations of producers of aquatic products" approved June 25, 1934 (15 U.S.C. 522) ; review of orders of petroleum control boards under section 5 of the Act entitled "An Act to regulate interstate and foreign commerce in petroleum and its products by prohibiting the shipment in such commerce of petroleum and its products produced in violation of State law, and for other purposes", approved February 22, 1935 (15 U.S.C. 715d) ; actions for fines, penalties, or forfeitures under part V of title IV of the Tariff Act of 1930 (19 U.S.C. 1581–1624), or under the Anti-Smuggling Act (19 U.S.C. 1701–1711); criminal libel for condemnation, exclusion of imports, or other proceedings under the Federal Food, Drug, and Cosmetic Act (21 U.S.C. 301–392) ; disputes between seamen under sections 4079, 4080, and 4081 of the Revised Statutes (22 U.S.C. 256–258) ; habeas corpus under sections 2241–2254 of title 28, United States Code; motions to vacate, set aside or correct sentence under section 2255 of title 28, United States Code; actions for penalties for refusal to transport destitute seamen under section 4578 of the Revised Statutes (46 U.S.C. 679) ; actions against the United States under the Act entitled "An Act authorizing suits against the United States in admiralty for damage caused by and salvage service rendered to public vessels belonging to the United States, and for other purposes", approved March 3, 1925 (46 U.S.C. 781–790) , as implemented by section 7730 of title 10, United States Code.

COMMENT: Rule 1101 was amended by the Congress in several respects, most of them minor.

Subdivision (a) as submitted to the Congress omitted the Court of Claims and the commissioners of that court in enumerating the courts and judges to which the rules of evidence apply. At the request of the Court of Claims, the House Committee amended the rule to include the court and its commissioners within the purview of the rules.

Subdivision (b) is, according to the Advisory Committee, a combination of the language of the enabling acts with respect to the kinds of proceedings in which the making of rules is authorized.

Subdivision (c) was amended by Congress to conform with the action of Congress in replacing the several rules of privilege submitted by the Supreme Court with a single privilege rule. Subdivision (d), the Advisory Committee made clear, is not intended as an expression as to when due process or other constitutional provisions may require an evidentiary hearing, nor does it deal with the evidence required to support an indictment.

Rule 1102. Amendments

Amendments to the Federal Rules of Evidence may be made as provided in section 2076 of title 28 of the United States Code.

COMMENT: This rule was not included among those submitted by the Court. The rule submitted by the Court as 1102 now appears as 1103.

Rule 1103. Title

These rules may be known and cited as the Federal Rules of Evidence.